SCANDINAVIA IS a region of extremes—whe[...]
meets rugged wilderness, and perpetual winter nights are followed by
endless days of summer—and *Fire and Ice* proves that Scandinavian
cuisine is no exception. Founding editor of *Gastronomica* and the
West's leading culinary authority on the cuisines of the European
North, Darra Goldstein explores the rich cultural history and culinary
traditions of Denmark, Finland, Norway, and Sweden. From the bold
aroma of smoked arctic char to the delicate flavor of saffron buns,
and from the earthy taste of chanterelle soup to the fragrant aroma of
raspberry-rose petal jam, this beautifully curated cookbook features
over 100 inspiring and achievable recipes that introduce home cooks
to the glorious and diverse flavors of Nordic cooking.

FIRE
+
ICE

Dana Goldstein

FIRE+ICE

CLASSIC NORDIC COOKING

DARRA GOLDSTEIN

PHOTOGRAPHY BY STEFAN WETTAINEN

TEN SPEED PRESS
BERKELEY

introduction

At the water's edge in an old warehouse district of Copenhagen, I stand muffled in gray—not fifty shades, but a decent handful. The sky is leaden, with clouds the color of slate. Oil slicks spread across zinc-colored water, silvery puddles mottle concrete. Granite stones are dark with soot. The steel hulk of an unfinished bridge rises up over the canal. It's November, and there's no sign of the Little Mermaid, or of Tivoli's pleasure gardens. Pelting rain evades my umbrella. I try to shake the gloom by imagining this dock a few hundred years ago, when the Danish East India Company sent ships out to sea loaded with barrels of precious salt herring, or awaited their return with coveted spices—ginger and cinnamon, allspice, cardamom, and cloves. First making their way into gingersnaps and mulled wine, these flavors soon claimed a place in the Nordic kitchen.

On this rainy day there's little movement anywhere. As I gaze out toward the sea, once a lifeline to the world, it seems fitting that Copenhagen is again rocking the world, now with a modern-day export. For it's here, on this dock, in a restored eighteenth-century warehouse, that the restaurant Noma introduced New Nordic cuisine to the world, making Copenhagen a culinary powerhouse. I approach the warehouse the way I imagine princesses once approached magical kingdoms, with a frisson that could be awe or trepidation. Maybe it's both. A reservation at Noma is the holy grail of foodie pilgrimage. What if I don't like what I find?

Nature's gray palette slips inside the old building with me, except here it's transformed from chill into warmth, the hard surfaces of stone offset by softly glowing wood and fur throws aligned over the backs of chairs. Everything is uncluttered and understated, following the principles of modern Scandinavian design—an honest use of natural materials like wood, leather, stone, fur, and linen, an approach that privileges function even as it yields gorgeous form. The early twentieth-century ideology of "everyday goods of greater beauty" spills over into Noma's kitchen and finds its apotheosis on the restaurant's menu, where the food of survival is recast as stunning, innovative dishes that emphasize the wild taste of the North. If the flavors of local food are fresh and often subtle, New Nordic's are concentrated, with strong elements of mineral and brine. It's all about identity of place expressed in nature and transmuted onto the plate. Trees in temperate climes may bear luscious fruits, but the underappreciated gifts of the North are also beautiful: the aromatic sap, shoots, needles, and bark of birches and pines; the blue-black aronia berries; the sea buckthorn berries like edible gold. Nordic taste is anything but bland.

New Nordic is in many ways old, informed by the traditions of people who have learned how to live under severe conditions. Sami reindeer herders gathered protein-rich lichen and dried it long before it appeared as deep-fried reindeer lichen with mushroom powder on Noma's menu, where it sits evocatively on a bed of green moss garnished with a stone and a twig, enhanced with a dollop of birch-infused crème fraîche. Just about everyone picks black currants, elderflowers, and rose petals in season, though before Noma no one thought to put them together in a single tour de force bite called "blackcurrant berry and roses"—black currant fruit leather shaped into balls and filled with cultured cream, then garnished with pickled rose petals, elderflower blossoms, and pollen. The purest flavors are the freshest, and Nordic foodways have always—necessarily—celebrated both the seasonal and the organic. Summer meadows, forests, and bogs spill over with berries, including prized cloudberries and arctic bramble. Spring offers up pine shoots and tiny birch leaves, fall brings mushrooms and game. Year-round the

rivers, lakes, and sea provide herring and mackerel, vendace and salmon, all high in healthy omega-3 fats. The Scandinavians have long recognized these foods as rich sources of vitamins, as are the whole grains of their hearty porridges and breads and the root vegetables on their winter tables. And yet, although berries are rich in antioxidants and spruce shoots burst with vitamin C, it's not micronutrients that the Scandinavians seek. They crave the vitalizing tastes, the earthy potency that these foods provide, whether they have been foraged, cultivated, or caught.

The Nordic palate represents a northern way of thinking—a creativity fostered by austerity. When snow covers the ground for eight months of the year, you can't just step outside to pluck fruit from trees or harvest produce. You need to plan ahead, to gather the bounty of forest and field during summer's fleeting warmth and put it up, not only to ensure survival but also to allay boredom. Late summer's lingonberries can be cooked into jam, but more often Scandinavians stir them raw with sugar, the berries' natural benzoic acid acting to preserve them. One spoonful of *rårörda lingon* (lingonberries) in the depths of winter is all it takes to bring a dazzling taste of summer rushing back. Similarly, reindeer loin can be dried into jerky or, better yet, buried fresh in the snow then shaved while still frozen into a cauldron, where its icy crystals melt into a rich, savory broth. And while beets can always be boiled, why not roast them in the embers of a fire to bring out their sweet, smoky flavor?

For me, the Nordic region has always been a place of intensities. I first traveled there forty years ago, on the verge of the summer solstice. As a near-penniless college student I'd taken a cheap flight to Finland that landed me in Helsinki at midnight. I remember exiting the plane's dim interior into an astonishing half-light, a subtle yet radiant glow like a waking dream. For a moment I felt more disoriented than if I'd stepped out into pitch darkness—at least then I would have had my midnight bearings. But I soon gave myself over to the mysterious light—the fabled midnight sun—and the surprising forms its shadows cast. I no longer recall how I made my way to the hostel or how I made myself understood at a time when few Finns spoke English, but the quality of that light has stayed with me all these years—as has the memory of the wondrous breakfast I woke up to the next morning. Fresh rhubarb compote with heavy cream, rye porridge, light-as-air lingonberry pudding, barley bread inflected with fennel and anise seed, each flavor a small explosion on my tongue.

I started finding my bearings as autumn hurtled into December and the days grew dark. It was then that I began to understand what else the North is about. Yes, there's the seasonal contrast—the glorious midnight sun and the often-oppressive dark. But there's so much more to the North than the (literal) polar opposites. Pristine ice—cold's purest reflection—hardens into a brilliance that shines blue. The aurora borealis illuminates winter's black skies. Golden gingerbread and bright yellow saffron buns mark Christmas and St. Lucia's Day. Candles flicker in the darkness, on tables, on trees, in windows in both the city and the countryside. The Nordic solution to a harsh climate is to embrace it. Much as my friends anticipate the summer, dreaming of the basketfuls of mushrooms and berries they'll forage, they're equally keen to camouflage themselves in white, strap on white-painted skis, and glide silently through the winter landscape in search of capercaillie and black grouse. Both ice and fire ensure survival, from the simple freezing of food to its roasting and smoking. Ice-cellar salmon, frost-bump beef, fire-glow salmon, ash-baked celery root—all of these dishes are practical yet ingenious responses to what would otherwise be the dull ache of need.

Preservation techniques underlie the Nordic diet. Curing, culturing, drying, and fermenting are all commonly practiced throughout the North. While the much-mocked lutefisk—cod preserved with lye and then reconstituted before boiling—may indeed be an acquired taste, why not celebrate the inspired excellence of Norway's other dried fish? *Tørrfisk* is dried on poles in the salt air, the more delicate *klippfisk* on the large, flat rocks edging the sea. Or my own favorite, *boknafisk*, semidried cod that poaches to a silken consistency.

Preserving creates intensity, concentrating flavors through drying or enhancing them with vinegar or salt. Soaking lamb in whey or buttermilk for days tenderizes the meat and allows it to remain fresh longer, but it also adds a touch of piquancy. The sharpness of salted and pickled foods seems perfectly designed to complement distilled spirits like aquavit, and the beer that for centuries has provided Scandinavians with an important source of carbohydrates (as well as an alcoholic kick!). Anyone who considers Nordic food plain as potatoes need only taste Jansson's Temptation (page 207), in which salty-sweet Swedish anchovies melt into a rich mixture of potatoes and cream. Local connoisseurship is also evident in the many forms of salting, from a light overnight cure of duck breasts rubbed with allspice, pepper, and salt to more complex, fermented foods that

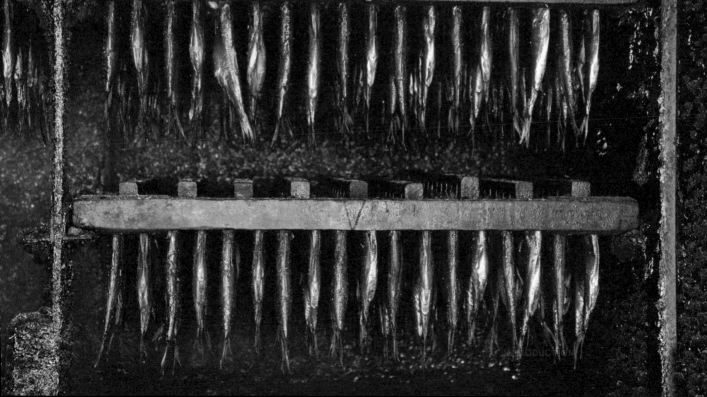

are the stuff of Anthony Bourdain-style adventuring—Sweden's *surströmming*, or fermented herring, and Norway's *rakefisk*, fermented trout. Though noses may turn up at these pungent types of fish, *surströmming* and *rakefisk* are for some people great delicacies, extreme iterations of a frugal technique meant to minimize expenditure on imported salt. They exist at the distant end of a continuum that begins with the far more familiar gravlax, found throughout the Nordic lands—lightly cured salmon so exquisite in flavor that it's a fixture at the finest gatherings. This dish similarly arose from thrift. Short for *gravad lax*, or "buried salmon," the name refers to the fishermen's practice of preserving their catch by burying it in the sand. Today, gravlax is made in the home kitchen and seasoned in all sorts of inventive ways: with white pepper and allspice, elderflowers and lemon, aquavit or vodka. An abundance of fresh dill gives the salmon its distinctive northern flair. Sliced ultrathin and sometimes shaped into rosettes, gravlax epitomizes the evolution of Nordic food from a cuisine of practicality to one of playfulness and verve.

My studies and my travels have taken me from Finland and Sweden to Norway and Denmark (and back, many times). In each country I discovered commonalities— a love for cured and salted fish, for game, for pickled vegetables and roasted roots, for flavors like dill, allspice, juniper, cardamom, and clove—that come together in a spectrum we can identify as Nordic. But I also discovered extraordinary regional dishes tied to local identities, such as the egg-rich pies of Finnish Karelia, the reindeer stew of Swedish Lapland, the beer-infused crackers of Ålesund, Norway, and the dark, sweet malt bread of the Åland Islands. Cooking practices know no political boundaries, especially for the Nordic countries, whose histories are so entwined. All of Scandinavia was united under a single rule with the signing of the Kalmar Treaty, which lasted for more than a century, from 1397 to 1523. Nordic culinary culture reflects this shared history in its use of fish, grains, dairy, and spices. But some of the most distinctive dishes, like Västerbotten cheese pie and apple soup with juniper, remain specific to a certain locale. As you read through the recipes in this book—classic Nordic home cooking with a touch of the new—you'll see that I've named them both in English and in Swedish, Danish, Norwegian, or Finnish. My choices reflect the place where that dish is most traditional, or where it resonated most for me as I drew on memories of extraordinary meals I've shared with Nordic friends over the years.

As a personal footnote, I was surprised to discover in testing these recipes that even older memories began to surface. Making Swished Cucumbers (page 102), I suddenly recalled my excitement when my parents hosted the Finnish minister of social affairs and his wife on their visit to Pittsburgh, just weeks after I turned six. Visitors from afar! I dug out the gifts they brought my sister, my brother, and me—dolls in native dress, two girls and a boy. Their limbs are now disfigured, and one girl is partially dismembered. But, astonishingly, the boy's miniature *puukko*—his curved hunting knife—remains intact in his belt. Norway also came back in a flash as I opened a can of sardines. I remembered my first semester in college, watching friends gleefully unpack shoe boxes of dark chocolate brownies and chocolate chip cookies, while I gazed down at my own care package of Norwegian King Oscar sardines, the first shipment of the one hundred cans that my mother had won as first prize in the company's recipe contest. Though the sardines are long gone, the other half of her prize, a beautiful pewter bowl hand-hammered with patterns of Viking ships, still gleams in my pantry.

Perhaps the most surprising connection to things Nordic in my past occurred as I was completing this book. In a secondhand store I happened upon an old jelly spoon, whose pattern I recognized as the silver plate from my childhood. I still have a few pieces scattered in my drawers, including the four-inch-long baby fork that I used for my own daughter. But I had never thought to learn the pattern's provenance. I felt giddy to discover that Lillian Helander, the daughter of Swedish immigrants and one of the few women working in a then largely male profession, had designed the pattern in 1938. Its name? Danish Princess. Clearly my love of the North was ordained! I'd been lovingly fed a Scandinavian aesthetic from my first solid bites.

A NOTE ON INGREDIENTS

Most of the ingredients called for in this book are readily available in grocery and health-food stores. Others, like elderberry flower concentrate and salted herring, can be ordered efficiently from the online sources listed in the back of the book.

Unless otherwise noted, all recipes use unsalted butter and kosher salt. The flour is unbleached all-purpose. Eggs are always farm fresh and graded large.

APPETIZERS

ROASTED OYSTERS WITH FRESH CHEESE...15

SHRIMP TOAST...17

BEET TARTARE...19

CURED DUCK BREAST...20

VÄSTERBOTTEN CHEESE PIE...22

EGG SALAD WITH SWEDISH ANCHOVIES...25

DILL-MARINATED HERRING...26

CHOPPED HERRING SPREAD...28

LIVER PÂTÉ...29

WHITEFISH TARTARE...30

CURED HERRING
WITH MUSTARD MAYONNAISE...32

BEET TERRINE
WITH HORSERADISH CREAM...33

SOS may be the universal cry for help, but it carries a different kind of urgency in Sweden, where the letters also stand for *Smör, Ost, och Sill*—butter, cheese, and herring. Or, as my friends prefer to render it, *Snaps, Ost, och Sill*—schnapps, cheese, and herring, a guaranteed restorative. The Nordic countries are home to an astonishing arsenal of beers, ales, and the caraway-flavored spirits known as aquavit. Beverages both hopped and distilled provide perfect foils for the piquant, salty flavors that characterize Nordic appetizers, most visibly displayed on the lavish buffet known as the *smörgåsbord*. This Swedish way of eating dates back to the eighteenth century. Before then Swedes enjoyed a *brännvinsbord* (distilled spirits table), which emphasized alcoholic spirits. The smorgasbord features food. The word *smörgås* (literally "butter goose") is a colorful term for the clumps of butter that appeared on the surface when cream was churned and whose lively movement made people think of running geese. The word eventually came to be used for a butter-spread sandwich, and then for the table (*bord*) on which it appeared alongside many other dishes. Cold dishes predominate on the smorgasbord, especially fish and herring, which for the most lavish spreads can appear in up to sixteen different ways, cured, pickled, and smoked.

The Danish *smørrebrød*, or open-faced sandwich, is equally distinctive and diverse. The simple sandwiches of the past became towering works of art in the late nineteenth century when they were served at the fashionable restaurant Nimb in Copenhagen's Tivoli Gardens. Today's open-faced sandwiches run the gamut from sweet bay shrimp or fried eggs to roast beef or liver pâté, all garnished with pickled or fried vegetables to create contrast in texture and flavor.

True to Nordic taste, the appetizers in this chapter focus on fish, and show the extraordinarily diverse flavors that can be coaxed from ordinary ingredients. But no matter which appetizer you choose, be sure to have some cheese and crispbread on hand. And don't forget the schnapps!

ONE OF MY favorite food memories is of walking out onto the mudflats on the island of Fanø on Denmark's west coast, with my friend Eja and oysterman Jesper Voss on a chilly November morning. Jesper carries a permit to dig the thousands of oysters that poke up out of the mud. Never have I seen so many oysters for the taking—to me it looked like paradise. But the Danish government is not so happy. These Pacific oysters were introduced for aquaculture in the 1980s and within a decade were displacing the beloved native blue mussels. Despite their abundance, the Danish government won't allow commercial harvesting, so Jesper takes individuals out to forage for their own.

Once our buckets were so full we could barely lift them, Jesper set up a grill on the beach, and we had an oyster feast for breakfast. Jesper placed the oysters, still in their shells, on the grill, and they popped open within a few minutes. Some he topped with a mignonette of vinegar, sugar, and shallots. Others he finished with a creamy cheese, as in the recipe here. After placing a dab of cheese on each oyster, Jesper threw a few sprigs of dried heather onto the fire and let the oysters smoke for a minute. Jesper used a local cheese flavored with ramps, but a triple-cream cheese made by Valfraisor the firmer Boursin, would also work. I've adapted Jesper's grilling technique for the oven.

Ristede østers med friskost

 # ROASTED OYSTERS
WITH FRESH CHEESE

MAKES AS MANY OYSTERS AS YOU AND YOUR FRIENDS CAN EAT

Rock salt

Fresh oysters

Garlic and herb spreadable cheese, such as Valfrais or Boursin

Finely chopped fresh chives, for garnish (optional)

Place a thick layer of rock salt in a heavy baking sheet with sides. Place the sheet in the oven and preheat to 425°F.

Meanwhile, scrub the oysters. When the oven is ready, remove the sheet and place the oysters on the hot salt, curved side down. Roast the oysters until the shells open, about 6 minutes. Remove the sheet from the oven and carefully pry off the flat shells to reveal the plump oysters inside. If any oysters remain unopened, return them to the oven to roast another minute or two; if they still fail to open, discard them.

Top each oyster with a dab of soft cheese—about ½ teaspoon per oyster—and return them to the oven for a couple more minutes.

Garnish with chives, and serve immediately.

VARIATION: The oysters can also be cooked on a charcoal or propane grill. Cover the grill and roast the oysters until they pop open, then dab with cheese and return to the grill until the cheese softens, a couple of minutes more.

TOAST SKAGEN

Toast Skagen is my Proustian dish, transporting me back to Stockholm and newlywed bliss. I learned to make this stunning appetizer from fishmonger Tommy Henriksson of Melanders Fisk in Stockholm's great food market, Östermalms Saluhall. Just married and living on a stipend in what was then one of Europe's most expensive cities, my husband and I usually shopped at the cheapest local supermarket, the ICA. But we couldn't resist the food hall and its enticing displays. Our weekly excursion to the Saluhall was like visiting a museum, especially during wildfowl season, when the gorgeous plumage of ptarmigan, capercaillie, and hazel grouse created abstract canvases in shades of earth and snow.

Tommy must have noticed how often we appeared at his stand, gazing longingly at the fish and shellfish on offer, because before too long he took us under his (unfeathered) wing and began to introduce us to the bounty of Swedish waters. Thanks to Tommy we learned the joys of fresh herring, of sweet, tiny bay shrimp, of golden *löjrom*, or vendace roe.

I assumed at first that shrimp toast was something our friend Tommy invented for us–figuring that even grad students could afford a little bay shrimp and a gram of vendace roe. But I soon learned that *Toast Skagen* is one of Sweden's most iconic dishes, even though it is less than sixty years old. As the story goes, the famous Swedish gastronome Tore Wretman, owner of the exclusive Restaurang Riche in Stockholm, was sailing in a regatta near Skagen, Denmark, a fishing port on the Jutland peninsula's northern tip. His boat was not doing well and his crew was disheartened, so Wretman disappeared into the galley to see what he could rustle up. There he found bread, eggs, oil, shrimp, fish roe, lemon, and dill (this was a Swedish boat, after all). Attuned to the French-inspired food of his restaurant, Wretman used the oil and eggs to make a classic mayonnaise to bind the shrimp. But when asked what his concoction was called, he didn't miss a beat: "Skagen." The dish soon appeared on Riche's menu and spread throughout the culinary world.

ALTHOUGH TOMMY MADE his version with mayonnaise and chile sauce (see opposite), I prefer to let the delicate flavor of the shrimp shine through, adding only some minced onion for piquancy and lightening the dressing with a little crème fraîche. Small, sweet shrimp are best for this dish. I like the tiny bay shrimp from Maine, but if you only have access to larger shrimp, boil them a bit longer, according to size, and chop them before mixing with the dressing. Sadly, we can't get *löjrom* in the States. Since 2010, when the vendace roe from Kalix in Sweden's far north received Protected Designation of Origin status from the European Union, international demand has far exceeded supply. But domestic whitefish roe makes a fine substitute.

You can make the shrimp mixture several hours in advance and keep it chilled. Assemble the toasts just before serving.

Toast Skagen

SHRIMP TOAST

SERVES 4 TO 6

1 pound peeled bay shrimp

3 tablespoons mayonnaise

3 tablespoons crème fraîche or sour cream

2 tablespoons minced red onion

¼ cup minced fresh dill, plus 16 dill sprigs

2½ teaspoons freshly squeezed lemon juice

¼ teaspoon salt

Freshly ground white pepper

8 slices soft white bread

2 tablespoons butter, at room temperature

2 ounces whitefish roe

Bring a large pot of salted water to a boil. Add the shrimp and cook for 2 minutes, no more, so that they remain firm. Drain and immediately run under cold water to stop the cooking.

In a bowl, stir together the mayonnaise, crème fraîche, onion, minced dill, lemon juice, salt, and pepper. Stir in the shrimp. Cover and let sit for 30 minutes for the flavors to meld.

Remove the crusts from the bread and cut each slice in half. Butter the bread on both sides and brown lightly in a skillet over medium heat. Transfer the toasts to a serving platter and top each toast with a generous spoonful of the shrimp mixture. Garnish with a dollop of whitefish roe and a dill sprig.

VARIATION: Top buttered baked potatoes with this mixture instead of serving it on toast.

THERE'S NO TYPO here! This ruby beet tartare is a vegetarian take on the classic *råbiff* introduced to Sweden from France in the nineteenth century. Like many salads, it's most dazzling in summer, when beets are sweet and garden fresh. Winter beets will yield a darker garnet dish, not quite so brilliant, and you may want to add a little sugar to perk it up. Spread these beets on bread or crackers, plate them with cured fish or meat, or scoop them onto a bed of lettuce. The flavor is beautiful at any time of year.

Tartar på rödbeta

BEET TARTARE

MAKES ABOUT 2 CUPS

1½ pounds beets

1 by ½-inch piece horseradish, peeled and chopped

1 tablespoon cider vinegar

1 small shallot, coarsely chopped

2 tablespoons coarsely chopped dill pickle

1 tablespoon mayonnaise

2 tablespoons minced fresh dill

¼ teaspoon salt

Freshly ground pepper to taste

Bring a large pot of salted water to a boil. Add the beets and cook until tender, 30 to 45 minutes, depending on their size and age. Drain, peel, and chop coarsely.

In a mini food processor or spice grinder, whir the horseradish with the cider vinegar until it is grated.

Place the beets in the bowl of a food processor. Add the grated horseradish mixture along with the shallot and pickle and process until finely chopped. Be careful not to make a puree—the tartare should be minced, with some texture.

Transfer the beets to a bowl and stir in the mayonnaise, dill, and salt. Season with pepper to taste. Cover and refrigerate for at least 2 hours before serving.

THIS RECIPE COULDN'T be simpler. Salt, sugar, and spices are rubbed into wildfowl that's left to cure overnight, with juniper berries accentuating the game's wild flavor. In Finland, black grouse would be the bird of choice, but I've discovered that moulard duck makes an excellent substitute. The meat benefits from a tart garnish of lingonberry or red currant preserves.

Riimiankanrintaa
 # CURED DUCK BREAST
SERVES 6 TO 8

8 ounces moulard duck magret (half breast)

2 large juniper berries

2 tablespoons salt

2 tablespoons sugar

½ teaspoon freshly ground pepper

⅛ teaspoon ground allspice

Lingonberry jam or red currant preserves, for serving

Remove the fat and any membrane from the duck breast. Crush the juniper berries in a mortar with a pestle.

In a small bowl, mix together the salt, sugar, pepper, allspice, and crushed juniper berries. Rub this mixture into the duck on both sides. Cover and cure the duck in the refrigerator for 12 hours.

Rinse the duck and pat dry with paper towels. To serve, slice the duck against the grain into very thin slices. Plate it with lingonberry jam.

VÄSTERBOTTEN IS A tangy cow's milk cheese from the northern Swedish region of Norrland, produced in limited quantities and therefore much prized. Aged for at least a year, the cheese is slightly crumbly and sharp, though it has a sweet edge. Västerbotten is delicious atop crispbread, but it's extravagantly good when baked into a rich, creamy pie. Variations of the pie, often served at August crayfish parties, are found throughout Sweden. Many online retailers stock Västerbotten (see page 284), but a good Italian Parmigiano-Reggiano or aged Cheddar can be substituted.

Västerbottenpaj

VÄSTERBOTTEN CHEESE PIE

SERVES 10 TO 16

CRUST

10 tablespoons butter, cut into pieces

1½ cups flour

½ teaspoon salt

6 to 7 tablespoons ice water

FILLING

3 eggs

1 cup heavy cream

2 tablespoons sour cream

8 ounces Västerbotten cheese, coarsely grated

Preheat the oven to 375°F.

To make the crust by hand, in a bowl, use a pastry blender or two knives to cut the butter into the flour and salt until it resembles coarse meal. Add 6 tablespoons of ice water all at once and work it in quickly with a fork, just until the dough holds together. The amount of water will depend on the humidity—you may need an extra tablespoon. Be careful not to overmix.

To make the crust in a food processor, place the butter, flour, and salt in the bowl of a food processor and pulse until the mixture resembles coarse meal, about 10 pulses. Add 6 tablespoons of ice water and pulse again, just until the dough holds together when pressed with your fingers. Add another tablespoon of water if necessary, but be careful not to overmix. Remove the dough from the food processor and shape into a disk.

On a floured surface, roll the dough out into an 11-inch round and fit it into a 9-inch tart pan with removable sides. Prick the dough all over with the tines of a fork. Place a sheet of aluminum foil on top of the dough and cover it with pie weights or dried beans to keep the dough from puffing up. Bake for 20 minutes. Remove the foil and pie weights, then bake until the crust is golden, about 12 minutes more.

Meanwhile, make the filling. In a bowl, lightly beat the eggs and stir in the heavy cream, sour cream, and, finally, the cheese. Pour the filling into the baked crust. Bake the pie until golden on top, about 25 minutes.

Serve at room temperature.

VARIATION: To make a chanterelle and cheese pie, while the crust is baking, clean and finely chop 8 ounces of chanterelle mushrooms. Melt 1 tablespoon of butter in a skillet over medium-low heat and add the mushrooms, 1/4 teaspoon of salt, and a few grindings of pepper. Sauté until the moisture released by the mushrooms evaporates, about 5 minutes. When the crust has baked, spread the mushrooms in an even layer over the bottom of the crust, then pour the cheese filling over them. Proceed with the recipe.

LIKE JANSSON'S TEMPTATION (page 207), this appetizer is often served late at night with cold beer and schnapps. Literally, the Swedish word *gubbröra* means "old man's mix"—the dish is so zesty that it will perk anyone up, even an old man, and is intended to enliven a party that's in danger of winding down. The kick comes from the Swedish anchovies (see Sources), which lend a salty-sweet tang. Soft-boiled eggs make the salad extra creamy and rich. This recipe comes from Mia Gahne, a marvelously talented food writer and stylist whose exquisite eye and playfulness are displayed in the photos of this book. Although *gubbröra* is usually served on dark bread or crispbread, it looks adorable when presented in eggshells, as Mia likes to do.

Gubbröra

EGG SALAD
WITH SWEDISH ANCHOVIES
SERVES 4

1 (4.4-ounce) can Swedish anchovies

1 small red onion, minced (about ½ cup)

1 tablespoon butter

4 eggs, at room temperature

½ cup finely chopped fresh parsley

Dark bread or crispbread, for serving (optional)

Freshly ground pepper to taste

1 (2-ounce) jar whitefish roe, for garnish (optional)

Finely chopped fresh dill or chives, for garnish

NOTE: If you want to present the *gubbröra* in eggshells, use an egg topper or sharp knife to cut a crosswise band through each shell so that you can use the half shells for serving. It's fine if the edges are a little jagged.

Drain the anchovies, reserving some of the brine, and chop them into small pieces. Set aside.

In a small frying pan over low heat, gently cook the onion in the butter for 3 to 4 minutes. When the onion softens, add the anchovies and stir until "melted," about 30 seconds. Stir in a little of the reserved brine. The amount of brine depends on how salty you want the dish to taste. Keep the mixture warm over very low heat.

Meanwhile, place the eggs in a pot and add enough water to cover. Bring to a boil, then lower the heat so that the water is simmering rapidly. Cook the eggs until the yolks are just set, about 5 minutes. Pour off the water from the pan and immediately run cold water over the eggs to stop further cooking.

Stir the parsley into the warm anchovy mixture. Crack the eggs and scoop them right into the pan, breaking them up with a rubber spatula.

Leave the mixture on low heat for a half minute or so, just long enough for it to warm through. Be careful not to overcook the *gubbröra* or the eggs will turn rubbery.

Spoon the *gubbröra* onto dark bread or crispbread, or serve it with a small spoon in eggshells (see note). Grind a generous amount of pepper onto each serving. If desired, top with a spoonful of whitefish roe. Garnish with finely chopped fresh dill or chives.

SCANDINAVIANS TAKE THE excellence of their pickled herring for granted, and it's not unusual for people to make it at home, following the basic formula of the 1-2-3 *lag* (solution) that calls for 1 part distilled vinegar to 2 parts sugar and 3 parts water. But here's the rub: Scandinavian vinegar is much stronger than the standard vinegar available in the States, which contains only 5 percent acetic acid. Called *ättika* in Swedish, Scandinavian vinegar has between 12 percent and 24 percent acidity (the 24 percent solution is advertised as good for cleaning too). So I've played around with proportions to try to capture that robust Nordic taste while making use of our weakling American vinegar. If you love pickled herring but have eaten it only from a jar, this recipe will delight you. Excellent salt herring fillets can be ordered online (see Sources).

Inlagd sill

 # DILL-MARINATED HERRING

MAKES 2 QUARTS

2 pounds salted herring fillets

1¾ cups distilled white vinegar

1½ cups water

1½ cups sugar

4 teaspoons white peppercorns

1 large red onion, thinly sliced

1 small bunch dill, chopped (about 1½ cups)

Rinse the herring. Place in a large bowl and add enough cold water to cover. Allow to soak at least overnight or up to 12 hours, changing the water once.

In a saucepan, bring the vinegar, water, sugar, and peppercorns to a boil, then remove from the heat and allow to cool.

Sterilize two 1-quart wide mouth Mason jars. (See sterilization instructions in Raspberry–Rose Petal Jam, page 271.)

Rinse the herring fillets and pat them dry with a paper towel. Cut them crosswise into 1-inch pieces.

Layer the onion, the herring, and some dill in the jars. Repeat until the jars are filled.

Pour the cooled marinade over the fish, making sure to cover it completely. Seal the jars and store in the refrigerator for 2 days before using. It will keep for about 2 weeks.

FINELY CHOPPED VEGETABLES that mimic luxurious fish roe are often called "caviar." Here herring stands in for the real thing, and in its own potent way it's utterly satisfying. You can use commercially prepared herring marinated in wine sauce to make this spread. Any mild mustard will do, but Swedish style—mild and slightly sweet—nicely offsets the herring's tang. Pair this spread with rye bread or crackers, or use it as a topping for boiled new potatoes.

Sillikaviaari

 # CHOPPED HERRING SPREAD

SERVES 6 TO 8

8 ounces marinated herring

2 small hard-boiled eggs, finely chopped

½ cup minced red onion

1 to 2 tablespoons finely chopped fresh dill

1 cup sour cream

1 tablespoon Swedish-style mustard

2 tablespoons capers, drained, chopped if large

Remove the herring from the marinade and pat dry with paper towels. Chop the herring into small cubes and place in a bowl. Stir in the onion, dill, sour cream, mustard, and capers until well incorporated.

WE GENERALLY CONSIDER pâté a luxury food, but its origins are far humbler. For Scandinavians, pâté was all about thriftiness and preservation—a delicious way to ensure that all parts of a slaughtered pig would be used and to have a product that would keep for a long time. This Norwegian recipe hints at people's more marginal existence in the past. It has none of the pork butt or other well-muscled cuts we usually find in other pâté recipes, and it uses a surprising amount of flour to bind the fat. Yet this pâté turns out as richly flavored as any made from more expensive ingredients.

Although Nordic pâtés are traditionally made with pork liver, I use chicken livers; either type will work. Swedish anchovies (brined sprats; see Sources) add a salty-sweet complexity. For an earthy tone, stir in some sautéed chopped wild mushrooms.

Serve the pâté on bread or crackers along with anything pickled, such as beets, onions, or cornichons. Lingonberry preserves are good too.

Leverpostei

LIVER PÂTÉ

SERVES 8 TO 10

8 ounces pork belly, rind removed and coarsely chopped

1 pound chicken livers

1 yellow onion, coarsely chopped

5 canned Swedish anchovies

½ cup flour

¼ cup half-and-half

2 eggs

¼ teaspoon ground allspice

¼ teaspoon dried thyme

1 teaspoon freshly ground pepper

1 tablespoon salt

Preheat the oven to 325°F. Line a 6-cup, 8½ by 4½ by 2½-inch loaf pan with plastic wrap, using enough so that it overhangs the edges. Bring a large pot of water to a boil over high heat and have a large baking pan ready.

In a food processor, finely grind the pork belly. Add the chicken livers, onion, and anchovies and pulse to finely grind. Add the flour, half-and-half, eggs, allspice, thyme, pepper, and salt and pulse until everything is mixed well. Pour the mixture into the prepared loaf pan; it will be rather loose.

Press down on the pâté mixture to force out any air bubbles and smooth the top. Bring the plastic wrap up over the top of the mixture and close it tightly. Cover the top of the pan with aluminum foil, sealing the edges. To make a bain-marie, place the loaf pan in a larger baking pan and pour boiling water into the baking pan until it's halfway up the sides of the loaf pan.

Bake the pâté for 1½ hours to 1¾ hours, until it is firm and a thermometer registers 160°F when inserted into the middle.

Remove the loaf pan from the water bath and allow the pâté to cool at room temperature. Refrigerate overnight. To serve, invert the pâté onto a platter and remove the plastic wrap.

THIS RECIPE COMES courtesy of Anna-Maija Tanttu, Finland's Julia Child. Her cookbook *Northern Flavours* is a love letter to cold climes. We tasted this lovely appetizer, served in small, crisp cups made of rye, at her house during a long summer afternoon of socializing and eating whitefish tartare, zander with crayfish sauce, and a chanterelle-pea puree. Dessert was an ethereal cloudberry parfait inflected with cardamom and layered with a whipped cream gelée.

If you can't find whitefish, you can substitute salmon. The cubes can be made larger to turn this dish into a salad, served on a bed of lettuce. Either way, remember to start preparing the dish a day before you plan to serve it.

Siikatartari

>>> WHITEFISH TARTARE <<<

SERVES 4 TO 6

SALTED FISH

1 pound skin-on whitefish fillets

1 tablespoon coarse sea salt

¾ teaspoon sugar

½ teaspoon coarsely ground white pepper

A handful of fresh dill (stems and fronds), coarsely chopped

TARTARE

1 teaspoon vegetable oil

1 large shallot, finely chopped

2½ tablespoons mayonnaise

½ teaspoon Dijon mustard

1 tablespoon freshly squeezed lemon juice

2 teaspoons finely chopped fresh dill

2 teaspoons finely chopped fresh chives

Freshly ground black pepper

To make the salted fish, rinse the fish and pat dry with paper towels. (You will likely have 2 fillets, but if the fishmonger has given you a single large fillet, simply cut it in half crosswise to get 2 pieces.) With tweezers, remove any small bones. Place one fillet, skin side down, in a 9 by 13-inch glass dish.

In a bowl, stir together the salt, sugar, and white pepper, and sprinkle half of this mixture over the whitefish fillet. Top with half of the dill, as though you are making gravlax.

Sprinkle a little of the remaining salt mixture onto the flesh side of the second fillet and place it, skin side up, on top of the other fillet. Sprinkle the top with the remaining salt and dill.

Cover the dish tightly with plastic wrap, place a weight on top to compress the fish, and refrigerate. Let cure for 24 hours.

Several hours before serving, while the fish is still curing, make the tartare. Heat the oil in a small frying pan over medium-low heat, add the shallots, and sauté until they just begin to brown, 3 to 4 minutes. Set aside to cool.

In a small bowl, mix together the mayonnaise, mustard, lemon juice, dill, chives, and black pepper to taste. Stir in the shallots.

Remove the fish from the refrigerator and wipe off the salt mixture. With a sharp knife, carefully remove the skin, then finely chop the fish into tiny cubes. Add the fish to the shallot mayonnaise and stir to coat. Refrigerate the tartare for several hours before serving.

ANOTHER HERRING RECIPE, you may ask? I can't help it! Herring is so delicious and healthful that when the fresh fish is in season, I go a bit crazy. Here in the Northeast we get Atlantic herring, usually in early June; those of you on the West Coast will find the herring's Pacific cousin in the wintertime. As for Scandinavians, they make a distinction between the Atlantic herring (*sill* in Swedish) and the smaller, less oily Baltic herring (*strömming*), though there's little genetic difference between them. Nurture trumps nature. How they're named and how they taste depend on where they swim, whether in the relatively warmer Baltic or the colder waters of the North Sea. Each variety has its fervid partisans.

You'll need to plan ahead for this recipe. Begin curing the herring the morning of the day before you plan to serve the fish. That evening, spread it with the mayonnaise, and then it will be ready for dinner the next night. The recipe can easily be doubled or even quadrupled.

Sinappisilakat

CURED HERRING
WITH MUSTARD MAYONNAISE

SERVES 2

1 pound fresh herring (about 4)

¾ cup water

3 tablespoons distilled white vinegar

3 tablespoons mayonnaise

1½ tablespoons Dijon mustard

⅛ teaspoon sugar

Salt and freshly ground white pepper

¼ cup chopped fresh dill

Dense rye bread or boiled new potatoes, for serving

With a sharp knife, remove the heads and tails of the fish. Slit the belly and remove the innards, then carefully peel off the backbone. Rinse the fish and pat dry with paper towels. Cut each herring in half lengthwise to make two fillets.

In a shallow nonreactive glass or ceramic dish, stir together the water and vinegar, then lay the herring fillets in the mixture skin side down. Cover and refrigerate overnight; the ideal curing time here is 12 hours.

Drain the fish, discard the marinade, and pat dry with paper towels. Wash out the dish and return the fillets to it, skin side down.

In a bowl, stir together the mayonnaise, mustard, sugar, and 2 tablespoons of the dill. Season with salt and pepper to taste. Spread the mustard mayonnaise on the top of each fillet. Cover the dish and refrigerate for another 24 hours.

When ready to serve, sprinkle the fish with the remaining 2 tablespoons of dill. Place a fillet on a slice of dense rye bread to make an open-faced sandwich, or serve with boiled new potatoes.

THIS RECIPE IS laborious and time consuming, but it's also one of the most beautiful dishes in the book: a shimmering mound of deep garnet gelatin. For many Americans, aspic may seem like something best suited for a Gilded Age dinner. But in Scandinavia, aspics make frequent appearances even today. Although Nordic aspics are often meaty—like Sweden's beloved *kalvsylta*, a jellied veal loaf—in this recipe a smoky meat stock envelops a surprise filling that includes beets and herbs. And for all of your labors you'll get two meals in one. You can slice the meat left over from making the stock and serve it with mustard.

Rødbedeterrine med peberrodscreme

BEET TERRINE
WITH HORSERADISH CREAM

SERVES 10 TO 12

1½ pounds small beets

4 cups Stock (see recipe, page 34)

2 envelopes (2 tablespoons) unflavored gelatin

¼ cup cold water

¼ cup finely chopped fresh dill

¼ cup finely chopped fresh parsley

1 tablespoon freshly grated horseradish

6 tablespoons minced dill pickles

Salt and freshly ground white pepper

Thinly sliced pork shank, reserved from making stock (see recipe, page 34)

Horseradish Cream, for serving (see recipe, page 35)

Preheat the oven to 350°F. Spread the beets in a roasting pan and bake until they are tender, about 1 hour. When cool enough to handle, peel and cut into ¼-inch slices.

Bring the stock to a boil, then lower the heat and simmer to keep warm.

In a bowl, soften the gelatin in the ¼ cup water, then whisk in ½ cup of the hot stock. Pour the gelatin mixture into the rest of the stock and heat gently, stirring until the gelatin dissolves. Transfer the stock to a heatproof container (I use a large Pyrex measuring cup) and refrigerate until it becomes thick and syrupy, about 2 hours. If you want to accelerate the process, divide the stock in half and refrigerate in two containers.

While the stock chills, mix the dill, parsley, horseradish, and pickles in a small bowl. Set aside.

Line a 6-cup, 8½ by 4½ by 2½-inch loaf pan with plastic wrap. Layer the bottom of the pan with half of the sliced beets. Sprinkle liberally with salt and a few grindings of white pepper. Top the beets with half of the herb mixture. Sprinkle on a little more salt and pepper. Then add a thin layer of the reserved sliced pork shank.

CONTINUED

BEET TERRINE WITH HORSERADISH CREAM
CONTINUED

When the stock has begun to thicken but has not yet firmed, pour about 2 cups of it over the beets and herbs. Place the remaining stock along with the loaf pan in the refrigerator for 10 minutes, until the gelatin has set lightly. Then carefully add another layer of beets on top of the gelatin in the loaf pan. Sprinkle with salt and pepper, and top with the remaining herb mixture and another thin layer of meat. Pour the remaining stock over the top. It should come nearly to the top of the pan.

Cover the pan with plastic wrap and refrigerate overnight, until the gelatin is completely set. To serve, invert the terrine onto a platter and remove the plastic wrap. Cut into slices and serve with horseradish cream.

STOCK

1 smoked pork shank or ham hock, about 2 pounds

8 cups cold water

2 carrots

2 celery stalks

1 handful parsley

1 yellow onion, quartered

12 black peppercorns

1 medium beet, peeled and grated

1/4 teaspoon salt

Freshly ground pepper

Place the pork, water, carrots, celery, parsley, onion, and peppercorns in a large stockpot. Bring to a boil, then lower the heat and simmer until the pork is very tender, about 2 hours. Let the meat cool in the stock for 1 hour, then strain the stock through a sieve into a large measuring cup. Discard the vegetables but reserve the meat. Measure out 4½ cups of the stock and refrigerate for several hours or overnight, until the fat rises to the surface and can be lifted off in a single sheet with a spoon. Save any remaining stock for another use.

While the stock is chilling, with a sharp knife shave some very thin slices of meat from the pork shank and chill until you're ready to assemble the terrine. If the meat is so tender that it falls from the bone, it's fine to have shreds rather than slices.

Pour the defatted stock into a clean pot and add the beet. Bring to a boil, lower the heat and simmer for 5 minutes, then strain and measure again. You should have around 4 cups of stock. If you're a bit short, add some of the reserved stock. Taste for seasoning, adding a little more salt if necessary (the need for additional salt will depend on how salty the meat was to begin with). The stock may be made in advance and stored in the refrigerator for up to 2 days.

HORSERADISH CREAM

1 cup crème fraîche

4 to 5 tablespoons freshly grated horseradish

Salt, freshly ground white pepper, and sugar to taste

This cream tastes best when made a bit ahead of time to let the flavors meld.

In a bowl, combine the crème fraîche and horseradish. Season with salt, pepper, and sugar to taste. Whisk gently until soft peaks form.

BREADS

"Better to have bread than gold," goes a Finnish saying. So precious was bread that even the crumbs were scraped from the table to be used again. Difficult growing conditions in the North meant that few grains flourished, and for centuries barley and oats predominated. (When those crops failed, bark bread was made from the inner bark of trees, especially pine.) Rye, spreading eastward from Russia, eventually became the favored grain of the North, thanks to its wholesomeness and deep flavor. Denmark's famous open-faced sandwiches are unthinkable without the dense *rugbrød* that provides the perfect vehicle for mile-high toppings.

The earliest Nordic breads were flatbreads, often made from leftover porridge or the spent grains from brewing. As rye, and eventually wheat, became more common, breads became more diverse, with each small region boasting its own specialties. Finnish bread culture is especially rich. In the eastern part of the country, sourdough rye—which came to be one of Finland's defining tastes—was traditionally baked once a week. In the western part, hardtack was more typical, with baking carried out only twice a year. The flat, ring-shaped loaves were strung on poles through their central holes and left to dry. These loaves sometimes turned so hard that they had to be shaved with a knife.

Only in the late nineteenth century did the beautiful repertoire of sweet coffee-table breads made of wheat flour develop, thanks to industrialization, which made this fine flour affordable to import. What glories came out of Scandinavian ovens then! Wheat flour enriched with butter, milk, and eggs was shaped into elaborate braids, wreaths, twists, and buns flavored with cardamom or cinnamon, filled with almond paste or jam, or studded with raisins or with candied fruits at Christmas. Children clamored for freshly baked buns with a glass of cold milk when they got home from school. This chapter presents some of my favorite sweet breads, along with savory breads made from barley, oats, and rye.

THESE NORWEGIAN GRIDDLE-BAKED flatbreads—a sort of Norwegian tortilla—come in a surprising variety, from soft to something approaching hardtack. Made with wheat, rye, or barley flour, they're perfect for eating out of hand or wrapping around fish or a hot dog—a favorite Norwegian treat. The version here, enriched with butter, milk, and potato, is a relatively modern iteration of the basic *lefse* of flour and water.

Making utterly thin *lefse* is an art, one I confess I haven't completely mastered yet. It helps to have a special grooved rolling pin and *lefse* stick for transferring the superthin dough from counter to griddle. But even if your *lefse* turn out a bit thicker than the Norwegian ideal (as mine sometimes do), they'll still be delicious. *Lefse* taste best when newly made, but the dough keeps well in the refrigerator.

Potetlefse

POTATO FLATBREADS

MAKES 4 BREADS, SERVING 2 TO 4

1 large russet potato, peeled

1 tablespoon butter, at room temperature

2 tablespoons whole milk

¼ teaspoon salt

½ cup barley flour

Bring a medium pot of salted water to a boil. Add the potato and cook until tender, 25 to 30 minutes. Drain and mash while hot.

In a bowl, combine the potato, butter, milk, and salt, beating well with a wooden spoon to eliminate any lumps. Stir in the flour until well incorporated. The dough will be firm. Knead it briefly in the bowl till smooth, then cover and refrigerate for at least 2 hours or up to 2 days.

When you're ready to cook the *lefse*, preheat an ungreased griddle or large cast-iron pan over medium-high heat. Divide the dough into 4 pieces. Work with one piece at a time, keeping the others refrigerated. Transfer the piece of dough to a floured surface. Generously flour a rolling pin and use gentle taps to roll the dough out as thinly as possible into a round that's about 8 inches wide. Do not press down on the dough as you roll, or it will come apart. It's a good idea to loosen the dough frequently from the surface by running a spatula under it. Keep both the work surface and the rolling pin well floured to make sure the dough doesn't stick.

Now comes the tricky part. Slide a metal baking peel or broad spatula under the dough round and carefully slide it onto the preheated griddle. Cook, flipping once, until the *lefse* is flecked with brown, about 6 minutes on each side. Immediately wrap the *lefse* in a dish towel so that it remains soft. Roll out and cook the remaining dough. Serve hot.

BARLEY FLOUR LENDS an appealingly nutty flavor to baked goods. It's also the grain that thrived most reliably in the short growing season and poor soil of Scandinavia. Besides being nourishing food, barley was considered to have medicinal value—home remedies for easing pain included applying a poultice of barley porridge to the skin. Because barley is low in gluten, wheat flour must also be added to the dough so that it will rise sufficiently. These wholesome rolls fill the kitchen with a wonderfully yeasty aroma as they bake. Serve them with a generous slathering of butter, either plain or juniper-flavored.

Rundstykker med bygg og rugmel

BARLEY ROLLS

MAKES 2 DOZEN ROLLS

1 package (2¼ teaspoons) active dry yeast

1¾ cups lukewarm water

4 tablespoons butter, melted

1 egg, lightly beaten

2 teaspoons salt

2 teaspoons coriander seeds, crushed

1½ cups barley flour

½ cup rye flour

4 cups flour

In a large bowl, stir the yeast into ¼ cup of the lukewarm water and let proof for 10 minutes, until bubbles appear. Then stir in the remaining 1½ cups of lukewarm water, along with the butter, egg, salt, and crushed coriander seeds. Add the barley flour, rye flour, and 3½ cups of flour, mixing well with a wooden spoon to form a soft, rather sticky dough.

To knead the dough by hand, turn it out onto a floured surface and knead until it springs back to the touch, 8 to 10 minutes, working in the remaining ½ cup of flour. Avoid adding more flour, or the rolls will be dry.

To knead the dough in a mixer, use a dough hook on low speed until the dough springs back to the touch, about 5 minutes.

Shape the dough into a ball, transfer to a large greased bowl, and turn it to coat the top. Cover and let rise in a warm place until the dough has doubled in bulk, about 1½ hours.

Preheat the oven to 425°F. Line 2 baking sheets with parchment paper. Punch down the dough and turn it out onto a floured surface. Cut or tear the dough into 24 pieces. Shape each piece into a round and place on a baking sheet. Let the rolls rise in a warm place, lightly covered with a clean dishtowel, until puffy, 25 to 30 minutes. Bake the rolls until the tops are pale brown, about 20 minutes.

THE FLATBREADS OF Scandinavia are so diverse that they carry distinct regional names. These unleavened breads can be delicate, almost paper-thin, or thick and crisp with all sorts of seeds, like caraway, poppy, and flax. They range from soft—meant for eating hot from the griddle or hearth—to nearly tooth-shattering hardtack, the survival bread of the past. They also vary in shape. Many Scandinavian crispbreads have a sizable hole in the center, for stringing on long poles near the stove to dry. Although crispbread is readily available, you have to seek out the traditional shapes.

This recipe is an adaptation of the unusual flatbread of Ålesund, a town on the west coast of Norway that's about 300 miles north of Bergen. It combines beer and rye bread to create a cracker with some of the living flavors of sourdough. The taste goes beautifully with cheese or cured meat or fish. It also makes an excellent nibble.

One of the fun things about this cracker is that it can taste different each time you make it, depending on the bread and beer you use, so it's a perfect recipe for experimentation.

Flatbrød av øl og rug

 # BEER AND RYE CRACKER

MAKES 2 ROUNDS, SERVING 4 TO 8

8 ounces preservative-free rye bread with seeds, torn into chunks

2 cups beer

2 tablespoons butter, at room temperature

½ teaspoon salt

Soak the bread in the beer for at least 8 hours or up to overnight. I like to leave the crust on the bread for more chew and to create a beautifully abstract texture, but if the crust is hard, be sure to tear it into very small pieces.

Preheat the oven to 325°F. Line 2 baking sheets with parchment paper. Drain the bread, discarding the beer. With your hands, squeeze out all of the excess moisture. Transfer the bread to a bowl and knead in the butter and salt—it will be a very wet mass.

Scoop half of the mixture onto each baking sheet. Moisten your palms with cold water and pat each mass into a very thin round, no more than ⅛ inch thick and about 11 inches wide. I find it helpful to gently press the rounds out from the center to the edges. Patch any holes that appear.

Bake the crackers until nicely browned and dry to the touch, about 35 minutes. Slide them onto racks to cool. Break into irregular pieces to serve. When kept in an airtight container, the crackers will remain crisp for several days.

VARIATION: Use preservative-free multigrain bread instead of rye.

CRISPBREAD VARIATIONS ARE found throughout the Nordic countries. This one is Swedish. I adapted the recipe from my friend Eja Nilsson's wonderful cookbook, *Vardagskök med svenska smakor* (*Everyday Cooking with Swedish Flavors*).

To create the bread's distinctive faceted texture, roll the dough out with a regular rolling pin and then with a special notched rolling pin called a *kruskavel*. Be sure that the dough is rolled out very thinly. It's a bit tricky to get the bread perfectly crisp, so I treat these like savory biscotti and put them back in the oven for a second baking.

These crispbreads are an excellent platform for soft or hard cheese, and for pickled or smoked fish. And they will keep forever—or at least until the Vikings return.

Knäckebröd

 RYE CRISPBREAD

MAKES 12

1 package (2¼ teaspoons) active dry yeast

1 cup plus 2 tablespoons lukewarm water

3½ cups coarse rye flour

1 tablespoon butter, at room temperature

1 teaspoon caraway seeds, crushed

½ teaspoon salt

In a large bowl, stir the yeast into the lukewarm water and let proof until bubbles appear, about 10 minutes. Stir in the flour, butter, caraway seeds, and salt until a dough forms. The dough will be firm but not stiff, and slightly tacky. Cover the bowl and let the dough rest for 30 to 45 minutes.

Preheat the oven to 475°F. Line 3 baking sheets with parchment paper. Divide the dough into 12 balls. Work with one ball at a time, keeping the others under a dish towel so they don't dry out.

Sprinkle a surface liberally with rye flour and roll out the dough into a very thin round that's about 6 inches wide and no more than ⅛ inch thick. With the notched rolling pin, roll over the round lightly to make the distinctive triangular pattern, or prick it all over with a fork. A little raggedness on the edges looks homemade, but you can trim them, if desired.

With a spatula, transfer the round to a baking sheet and cut out a hole in the middle with a 1½-inch round cookie cutter.

Bake the rounds until they just begin to color, about 10 minutes. Slide the rounds off the baking sheets and onto racks to cool.

Decrease the oven temperature to 250°F. Return the rounds to the baking sheets (they can now overlap on 2 sheets) and bake for 30 minutes more, until crisp.

WE TASTED THESE wonderful oatcakes high in the mountains of Norway, at Sæterstad Gård, a farm where Siri Kobberrød and her family raise goats and make fifteen different types of goat cheese, from caramelized *geitost*, which is soft and sweet, to a special goat's milk "coffee cheese" that's meant for drinking with coffee.

Siri was kind enough to give me her recipe for these oatcakes, which pair beautifully with cheese. But I prefer to eat them as wholesome cookies. They derive their lovely texture from hartshorn, or baker's ammonia. Don't be alarmed at the slight ammonia smell you may detect as they're baking. It dissipates quickly and doesn't affect the taste of the oatcakes.

Havrekjeks

OATCAKES

MAKES ABOUT 1 DOZEN

4 tablespoons butter, at room temperature

¼ cup sugar

1¼ cups rolled oats (not quick-cooking)

½ cup plus 2 tablespoons flour

2¼ teaspoons baker's ammonia

Pinch of salt

2 tablespoons whole milk

Preheat the oven to 400°F. Line a baking sheet with parchment paper.

In a bowl, cream together the butter and sugar. In a separate bowl, stir together the oats, flour, baker's ammonia, and salt. Add half of the oat mixture to the creamed sugar mixture and stir together. Stir in the milk and then the remaining oat mixture. With your hands, form the dough into a mass—it will be somewhat sticky.

Turn the dough out onto a floured surface and generously flour a rolling pin. Roll the dough out until it's ¼ inch thick. With a 3-inch cookie cutter, cut out rounds and place on the baking sheet, about 2 inches apart. Bake the oatcakes until they are brown on the edges, about 9 minutes.

THESE SMALL, RICH pies are a specialty of Karelia, which is historically the southeastern part of Finland, though much of the region was ceded to Russia following the 1939–1940 Winter War. The pies were traditionally filled with barley porridge or a mix of malted grains, usually barley, rye, or oats, that had been soaked, dried, and reconstituted—a laborious process. Once the price of rice dropped in the late nineteenth century, creamy rice porridge became the filling of choice and the traditional fillings largely disappeared. So distinctive are these pies that in 2003 the European Union granted them TSG (traditional specialty guaranteed) status, a designation that celebrates their authentic character.

Because the dough is unfermented, a thin crust is one secret to the pies' success. The other secret is to use finely milled rye flour. If you can find only coarse, stone-ground rye flour, whir it in the food processor before making the dough. Even with these precautions, Karelian pies still become hard after a few hours, which is why they are always dipped in a buttery milk mixture or brushed with butter. If you can resist eating the pies right away, cover them with a dish towel to keep them soft.

For an even creamier texture, the pies are topped with *munavoi,* or "egg butter," a mixture of mashed hard-boiled eggs and butter. In some parts of Finland, the pies are served with chopped smoked fish instead of egg butter, the local vendace being the favorite.

These little pies are admittedly labor intensive, but making them is a great activity for a snowy afternoon.

Karjalanpiirakkat

KARELIAN PIES

MAKES 10 SMALL PIES

½ cup plus 2 tablespoons medium rye flour

6 tablespoons flour

½ teaspoon salt

7 tablespoons whole milk

1 tablespoon butter, at room temperature, cut into small pieces

Rice Filling (see recipe, page 49)

Milk-Butter Dip (see recipe, page 49)

Egg Butter (see recipe, page 49)

To make the dough, in a medium bowl, mix together the flours and the salt. Stir in enough milk to make a sticky but firm dough, then work in the butter with your fingers.

Turn the dough out onto a floured surface and roll into an 8 by 12-inch rectangle that's no more than ⅛-inch thick. Fold the dough in quarters by folding in the short outer edges to meet in the middle, then folding the dough again as though you are closing a book. Turn the dough 90 degrees, then roll it out again into an 8 by 12-inch rectangle, as though making puff pastry. Repeat this folding, turning, and rolling process 1 more time.

CONTINUED

Fold the dough into quarters once again and roll it out into a 4 by 12-inch rectangle. Fold the dough in half lengthwise and then roll it out again into a narrow strip that's about 20 inches long and 2 inches wide.

Cut the strip into 10 equal pieces. Roll each piece into a ball, then flatten into a small disk. Let the disks rest, covered with a dish towel, for 10 minutes.

Preheat the oven to 450°F. Line a baking sheet with parchment paper.

To assemble the pies, roll each disk out thin into an oval about 5 inches long and 3½ inches wide. Place 1 to 2 teaspoons of the rice filling down the center of the oval, leaving ½ inch of dough uncovered all around the perimeter. Gently flatten the filling to compress it slightly.

With floured hands, pinch the edges of the dough together at the end closest to you to form a point. Work your way up the sides of the dough, crimping the edges decoratively between thumb and forefinger to create a border around the exposed filling. Bring the top edges together in a point to make an oval pastry with an upright, crimped pattern. As each pie is made, place it on the baking sheet. Continue making pies with the remaining rice filling and balls of dough.

Bake the pies for 10 to 12 minutes. They will not color much, but the tips of the dough will turn dark in spots. Remove from the oven and, using tongs, immediately dip each pastry into the milk-butter dip until coated on all sides.

Transfer the pies to a serving plate. Spoon a dollop of egg butter onto each pie and serve immediately.

To prepare the pies ahead of time, return the pies to the baking sheet after dipping them in the milk-butter mixture, and cover with a dish towel to keep them soft. Then reheat gently in the oven. Top with egg butter and serve immediately.

RICE FILLING

6 tablespoons water

6 tablespoons short-grain rice

1½ cups whole milk

¼ heaping teaspoon salt

In a small pan, bring the water to a boil. Add the rice and cook, stirring, over low heat for a few minutes until the water has been absorbed. Add the milk little by little, stirring constantly. It will take about 20 minutes for all of the milk to be absorbed. When cooked, the rice filling should be soft and creamy but still moist. Remove from the heat and stir in the salt. Let sit 15 minutes before using. (If you are making this filling early in the day, it will thicken upon standing. Warm up over gentle heat until it softens again.)

MILK-BUTTER DIP

3 tablespoons salted butter

6 tablespoons whole milk

In a wide saucepan over low heat, combine the butter and milk and stir until the butter melts. Keep warm.

EGG BUTTER

1 small egg

2 tablespoons salted butter, at room temperature

Salt

Place the egg in a small saucepan, add enough water to cover, and bring to a boil. Cook for 8 minutes, then drain and immediately run under cold water to cool. Peel the egg and set aside. Cream the butter, then mash in the egg with a fork. Using a hand mixer or immersion blender, whip the egg butter for a few minutes until soft and fluffy. Season with salt to taste.

MALT BREAD IS found mainly in the Finnish archipelago, on the country's west coast. It is also made in Finland's Åland Islands, where the spoken language is Swedish. There it's known as *skärgårdslimppa* (archipelago bread) or simply *svartbröd* (black bread). This island bread was baked into dense, dry loaves that would keep for several months on fishing and sealing expeditions. Over time, as tastes changed, and as wheat flour and syrup became affordable, malt bread evolved into today's sweeter, softer loaf. Yet it remains associated with fish, holding a tenured spot on the traditional "herring table" prepared regionally at Christmas, Easter, and Midsummer.

Rea Ahlström of Helsinki bakes malt bread for special occasions, and the version that follows is adapted from her recipe. She and her husband have a farm outside of Helsinki where they grow grain and raise Hungarian partridges. In addition to this malt bread, Rea is, by necessity, famous for her game cookery. As she explains, "My husband hunts a lot so I have nine freezers full of game—you name it, I have it."

The texture of this bread is somewhat heavy and moist, so it makes excellent toast. If you brush the loaf with a little molasses before taking it out of the oven, the crust takes on a gorgeous sheen.

Saaristoleipä

MALT BREAD

MAKES 1 LOAF

1¼ cups buttermilk

2 tablespoons active dry yeast

¼ cup molasses, plus ¼ teaspoon (optional)

⅓ cup diastatic malt powder

¼ teaspoon salt

2½ cups medium rye flour

1½ to 1¾ cups bread flour

Heat the buttermilk in a small saucepan over medium-low heat until lukewarm. Pour ¼ cup of the buttermilk into a large bowl, sprinkle the yeast over it, and let proof until bubbles appear, about 10 minutes. Stir in the remaining 1 cup of buttermilk, the ¼ cup molasses, malt powder, salt, and rye flour. Add 1½ cups of the bread flour, mixing well, and stirring in as much of the remaining bread flour as needed to make a firm dough.

Turn the dough out onto a floured surface and knead gently for a few minutes until smooth. Transfer the dough to a large greased bowl and turn it to coat the top. Cover and let rise in a warm place until the dough has doubled in bulk, about 2 hours.

Generously butter a 10 by 5-inch loaf pan. Punch down the dough and place it in the loaf pan. Let the dough rise in a warm place uncovered until almost doubled in bulk, about 30 minutes. Meanwhile, preheat the oven to 375°F.

Bake the bread for 1 hour. (If desired, after 45 minutes of baking, brush the top of the loaf with ¼ teaspoon of molasses, and then bake for 15 minutes more.)

Transfer the pan to a wire rack and run a table knife around the edges to make sure the bread doesn't stick. Let cool for 10 minutes and then remove the bread from the pan to finish cooling directly on the rack.

LUSSEBULLAR **CAN BE** formed into many shapes, some recalling Christian symbols, others heathen. The most traditional are *lussekatter*, or "Lucia's Cats," which with their raisins resemble two eyes on a golden background—not unlike those on St. Lucia's platter (see page 57). The buns can also be molded as figure eights, crowns, plaited wreaths, hearts, sheaves, and "golden wagons" that recall pagan solar wheels, while buns shaped as priest's locks, Christmas stars, crosses, and church doors take their inspiration from the Church rather than from nature. No matter the form, these luminous buns will add a bright touch to your table.

Lussebullar

SAFFRON BUNS

MAKES 18 BUNS

1 cup whole milk

8 tablespoons (1 stick) butter, cut into pieces

½ teaspoon saffron threads, crumbled

1 package (2½ teaspoons) active dry yeast

¼ cup lukewarm water

¾ cup sugar

1 egg, at room temperature, lightly beaten

½ teaspoon salt

4 to 4½ cups flour

2 tablespoons raisins

GLAZE

1 egg, lightly beaten

In a small saucepan, combine the milk and butter over medium-low heat, stirring until the butter melts. Remove immediately from the heat and stir in the saffron. Set aside to cool to lukewarm.

Meanwhile, in a large bowl, stir the yeast into the lukewarm water and let proof until bubbles appear, about 10 minutes. When the milk is lukewarm, stir it into the yeast, along with the sugar, egg, salt, and 4 cups of the flour, adding as much of the remaining flour as needed to make a soft dough—it will still be slightly sticky.

Turn the dough out onto a floured surface and knead until it is smooth and elastic, about 10 minutes, adding as little extra flour as possible. Transfer the dough to a large, lightly greased bowl and turn it to coat the top. Cover and let rise in a warm place until doubled in bulk, 1½ to 2 hours.

Line 2 baking sheets with parchment paper. Punch down the dough. Divide it into 18 pieces, and then divide each piece in half. Roll each half between your palms into a strand that's about 4 inches long. To make Lucia's Cats, place 2 strands together lengthwise, then turn each end in toward the center to make 4 coils. (Alternatively, you can make a simple S shape by coiling

CONTINUED

the ends of each strand in opposite directions.) For golden wagons (pictured on page 54), lay one strand over the other to form an X, then turn the 4 ends toward the center to form coils, as for Lucia's Cats. Transfer each bun to a baking sheet and press a raisin firmly into the centers of the coils. Repeat with the remaining dough. Cover the buns and let rise in a warm place until puffy, 30 to 40 minutes.

Preheat the oven to 400°F. Brush the buns with the beaten egg. Bake until golden, about 15 minutes.

LUCIA

Golden *lussebullar* buns bring light to the dark days of winter. Traditionally served on December 13, St. Lucia's Day, they are deeply symbolic. Just where their symbolism derives from, though, is a matter of debate, as Lucia appears in both Christian doctrine and pagan lore. Most people believe that *lussebullar* (saffron buns) commemorate the Christian martyr Lucia of Syracuse, whose eyes were gouged out before she was killed. In some tellings, she gouged them out herself rather than submit to a non-Christian suitor, but then her sight was miraculously restored. St. Lucia is further associated with light because of her name, from the Latin *lux*; medieval paintings often depicted her holding her eyes on a golden platter.

I'm more entranced by the pagan associations, which involve the summoning of light to destroy evil forces. Until the Gregorian calendar reform in the sixteenth century, December 13 was the longest night of the year, and like Halloween, it was a dangerous time, when unclean spirits were about. To keep them at bay, young people roamed noisily from house to house, caroling and mumming in exchange for symbolically shaped buns and other foods. Their commotions were also meant to rouse the sun, to awaken it from the year's greatest darkness. These pagan ideas were reinforced in Sweden thanks to the close etymologies of Lucia and Lucifer, and the belief that Lucia was Adam's first wife, who kept company with the devil and gave birth to the invisible "little people" who lived underground.

Not surprisingly, the Church didn't approve of this interpretation. With the rise of Lutheranism, the raucous revelry and pagan fires of Lucia Night were eventually replaced by young girls dressed in white wearing crowns of light in the form of candles. By the twentieth century this more orderly form of celebration had become well established, and even today, each December 13th, candle-crowned young girls dressed in white offer coffee and *lussebullar* (though the candles are now often battery-powered).

CARDAMOM IS COMMON throughout Scandinavia, where warm spices like cinnamon, allspice, ginger, nutmeg, and cloves are deeply appreciated, especially in the mulled wine and gingerbread of the Christmas season, when they fill the house with lovely smells and seem to counteract the biting cold. Thanks to the founding of the Danish East India Company in 1616 and the Swedish East India Company in 1731, these prized spices became increasingly available, and they now lend characteristic flavor to Nordic foods. The region's extensive repertoire of sweet breads would be unthinkable without cinnamon and cardamom.

When I lived in Finland, cardamom-scented *pulla* was my go-to treat, a daily fix from the local bakery as I walked to the university. After fortifying myself with a slice (or two) of *pulla* and a cup of rich hot chocolate, I felt ready to face the world, no matter the midday twilight or the blowing snow.

Your bread will taste as good as the cardamom you use, so make sure it's fresh. I like to get whole pods, peel off the papery husks, and pound the seeds in a mortar.

Pulla

 # CARDAMOM BRAID

MAKES 2 BRAIDS

1 package (2¼ teaspoons) active dry yeast

¼ cup lukewarm water

36 cardamom pods, or 2 teaspoons ground cardamom

½ cup sugar

1 cup whole milk, lukewarm

2 egg yolks, lightly beaten

6 tablespoons butter, at room temperature, cut into small, separated pieces

¼ teaspoon salt

4 cups flour

1 egg, lightly beaten, for glazing

Pearl sugar, for sprinkling

In a large bowl, stir the yeast into the lukewarm water and let proof until bubbles appear, about 10 minutes.

Meanwhile, peel the cardamom pods and crush them in a mortar with a pestle.

Stir the sugar, lukewarm milk, egg yolks, butter, salt, and cardamom into the yeast mixture. Add the flour, stirring vigorously to distribute the butter and form a soft dough.

To knead the dough by hand, turn it out onto a floured surface and knead until it springs back to the touch, 8 to 10 minutes. To knead the dough in a mixer, use a dough hook on low speed until the dough springs back to the touch, about 5 minutes.

Shape the dough into a ball, transfer it to a large greased bowl, and turn it to coat the top. Cover and let rise in a warm place until the dough has doubled in bulk, about 1½ hours.

Line a baking sheet with parchment paper. Punch the dough down and turn it out onto a floured surface. Cut the dough in half and shape each piece into 3 balls. With your hands, roll each ball into a strand about 15 inches long. Braid 3 strands together and place on the baking sheet. Repeat with the remaining 3 strands. Let the braids rise in a warm place, uncovered, until almost doubled, about 45 minutes.

Preheat the oven to 375°F. Brush the braids with the egg and sprinkle generously with pearl sugar. Bake them until golden, 20 to 25 minutes. Transfer to a rack to cool.

VARIATION: Leftover *pulla* can be turned into French toast, known in the Scandinavian languages as "poor knights." It is more often served for dessert than for breakfast, often accompanied with strawberries and whipped or ice cream. The texture is best when made with *pulla* that is already getting stale–which is, of course, why the dish was first invented.

CARDAMOM BRAID FRENCH TOAST
SERVES 2

2 tablespoons unsalted butter

1 egg

½ cup whole milk

Pinch of salt

4 slices pulla, at least 1 day old

Lingonberry jam, for serving

Whipped cream, for serving (optional)

Melt a little butter in a 10-inch frying pan over medium-low heat. In a shallow dish, lightly beat the egg with the milk and salt. One at a time, dip the slices of *pulla* into the egg mixture to coat both sides, then place in the pan. Cook until lightly browned on the bottom, for just a couple of minutes, then flip and brown the other side, a couple of minutes more. Serve with lingonberry jam and, if desired, whipped cream.

THANKFULLY, THE ART of baking is alive and well in Scandinavia, where coffee breaks are a cherished part of the day. I'm especially fond of the sweetened yeast breads made in all sorts of intricate shapes. The truth is, anything with almond paste makes me swoon, and this beautiful wreath is a particular favorite. During our penurious year in Stockholm we had two weekly indulgences: a visit to Tommy, our friend the fishmonger, and a pastry at Vete-Katten, a warren of small rooms where coffee was served in Royal Copenhagen china and most of the patrons (it seemed to us) were ladies of a certain age, all perfectly dressed and coiffed. This *konditori* is now less formal and the plates more pedestrian, but the pastries and breads remain spectacular. It's hard to decide which I like best: *kanelbullar* (soft cinnamon buns), *semlor* (tender cardamom buns filled with marzipan and whipped cream), the lavish *prinsesstårta* (sponge cake layered with pastry cream, raspberry jam, and whipped cream mounded into a dome and draped with pale green marzipan), or this delightful almond wreath. *Mandelkrans* tastes best when very fresh, but you can reheat it gently to serve the next day.

Mandelkrans

 # SWEDISH ALMOND WREATH

MAKES 1 LARGE LOAF, SERVING 8 TO 10

1 package (2¼ teaspoons) active dry yeast

4 tablespoons sugar

¼ cup lukewarm water

¾ cup whole milk, lukewarm

1 egg, at room temperature

6 tablespoons butter, at room temperature and cut into pieces

¼ teaspoon salt

3 to 3½ cups flour

FILLING

½ cup blanched almonds

3 tablespoons sugar

3 tablespoons butter, at room temperature

⅛ teaspoon natural almond extract

In a large bowl, stir the yeast and 1 tablespoon of the sugar into the lukewarm water and let proof until bubbles appear, about 5 minutes. Stir in the remaining 3 tablespoons of the sugar, the lukewarm milk, egg, butter, and salt. Add 3 cups of the flour, mixing well until a soft dough forms.

To knead the dough by hand, turn the dough out onto a floured surface and knead until it springs back to the touch, 8 to 10 minutes, adding up to ½ cup more flour if necessary. To knead the dough with a mixer, attach the dough hook and knead the dough at slow speed until it springs back to the touch, about 5 minutes.

Shape the dough into a ball, transfer to a greased bowl, and turn it to coat the top. Cover and let rise in a warm place until the dough has doubled in bulk, about 1½ hours. Punch the dough down and turn it out onto a floured surface. Set aside while you prepare the filling.

CONTINUED

SWEDISH ALMOND WREATH
CONTINUED

GLAZE

1 cup confectioners' sugar

2 tablespoons freshly squeezed orange juice

Pearl sugar, for sprinkling

To make the filling, in a food processor grind together the almonds and sugar until the nuts are very finely ground. Transfer to a bowl, add the butter, and stir until a mass forms. Stir in the almond extract.

Line a baking sheet with parchment paper. Turn the dough out onto a floured surface and roll out to a 12 by 18-inch rectangle. With a small spatula, spread the filling evenly over the entire rectangle. Starting at the long end, roll the dough up into a log. Transfer it to the baking sheet, seam side down. Bring the ends together to form a circle, pinching them tightly to seal.

With scissors, snip the dough two-thirds of the way through the circular log at 1-inch intervals. Gently turn each cut section on its side. Let the loaf rise in a warm place, uncovered, until almost doubled, about 45 minutes.

Preheat the oven to 375°F. Bake the bread until golden, 20 to 25 minutes.

Meanwhile, make the glaze by mixing together the confectioners' sugar and orange juice.

While the loaf is still warm, spoon the glaze over the loaf. Sprinkle with pearl sugar. Transfer carefully to a rack to cool.

THESE SAVORY, PUFFED pancakes are inspired by those served at Copenhagen's most famous restaurant, Noma, where they're filled with lovage, spinach, and parsley. Almost as soon as I got home I rummaged in my pantry to uncover the well-seasoned *æbleskiver* pan I've had since grad school, and which a fellow student generously gave to me, along with her grandmother's recipe.

Æbleskiver started out as apple fritters–the word literally means "apple slices"–but they evolved into the cute little pancakes we know today. They are made in a special pan with hollows that cause the pancakes to cook up plump and round. *Æbleskiver* are often filled with jam or prunes, and sprinkled with powdered sugar. Sometimes they're served unfilled, with lingonberry jam on the side. This savory version makes a great appetizer at dinner.

Æbleskiver med krydderurter

SAVORY PUFFED PANCAKES

MAKES 3 DOZEN PANCAKES, SERVING 6

1¾ cups whole milk

1 tablespoon butter, plus more for cooking

1 package (2¼ teaspoons) active dry yeast

¼ cup lukewarm water

2 eggs, at room temperature, lightly beaten

2 cups flour

1 teaspoon salt

FILLING

2 tablespoons minced shallot

1 tablespoon butter

½ cup finely chopped spinach

¼ cup minced fresh parsley

1 tablespoon minced fresh chervil

1 teaspoon minced fresh tarragon

¼ teaspoon salt

Freshly ground pepper to taste

In a small saucepan, combine the milk and butter over medium-low heat, stirring until the butter melts. Set aside to cool to lukewarm. Meanwhile, in a large bowl, stir the yeast into the lukewarm water and let proof until bubbles appear, about 10 minutes. When the milk is lukewarm, stir it into the yeast along with the eggs. Combine the flour and salt in a small bowl, then stir them into the yeast-milk mixture until a batter forms. Cover and let rise in a warm place until bubbly, about 1 hour.

Meanwhile, make the filling. In a small skillet over medium-low heat, sauté the shallot in the butter until golden, about 5 minutes. Stir in the spinach, parsley, chervil, tarragon, and salt, and mix well until a moist paste forms. Season with pepper. Set aside.

Preheat the oven to 200°F and have a baking sheet ready. Put a tiny dab of butter into each indentation of the *æbleskiver* pan and set over medium heat. Spoon a tablespoonful of batter into each indentation, then top with about ½ teaspoon of the filling. Cover with another spoonful of batter, making sure not to overfill. Cook until the pancakes are browned on the edges and bubbles appear on the surface, about 4 minutes. Turn them with a skewer and cook until puffed and brown, another 4 minutes or so. Serve hot. You can serve the pancakes as they're made or keep warm in the oven until all the batter has been used.

SWEDEN

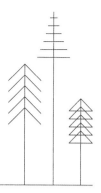

The two best known Swedish words in English may very well be *dynamite* and *smorgasbord*. The first, coined by its inventor, Alfred Nobel, entered English in 1867. The second took the U.S. by storm in 1939, dazzling visitors to the Swedish Pavilion at the New York World's Fair. Unfortunately, the word *smorgasbord* came to refer to any all-you-can-eat buffet, making most Americans more familiar with the workings of dynamite than with the true delights of a Swedish table.

And what delights there are! From saddle of reindeer with wild mushrooms to poached cod with dill and horseradish, from cloudberry soup to lingonberry parfait, Swedish food is a gorgeous blend of the earthy and refined. Because the country is so long, stretching from the Baltic to the Arctic, it blends numerous culinary traditions. The province of Skåne in the south (known as the "Tuscany of Sweden") is temperate enough to grow a multitude of crops, including wine grapes. The cooking there has much in common with that of neighboring Denmark, to which the region once belonged. Skåne is home to superfoods that exist at the extremes of sweet and sour and capture the flavor of land and sea: aromatic honey from blazing wildflower fields; and citrusy sea buckthorn from the coast, pressed into mouth-puckering drinks and sorbets. A thousand miles away, in the far northern reaches of Lappland, snow lingers well into May. There, Swedish, Finnish, and Sami food cultures mingle, making foraging and hunting a natural part of life. Slightly south and to the east, in the microclimate of Tornedal on the border with Finland, the soil is marvelously rich in minerals from the Torne River and the nearby fells. During the season called *varmvinter* (warm winter), which lasts from March into May, the hours of daylight are long, giving a boost to early spring vegetables even as the river and Bothnian Bay remain frozen and still. The locals also eagerly await the annual whitefish run, when thousands of silvery fish leap and twist in the rapids at Kukkolaforsen, to be caught in old-fashioned weirs and served fresh, salted, or smoked. In Kiruna, two hundred miles northwest, shiitake mushrooms are cultivated in the world's largest iron-ore mine, so that fresh mushrooms can be enjoyed even when wild ones can't be gathered. Add to this two thousand miles of coastline, and it's easy to see why shellfish are also important to the traditional Swedish diet.

Until fairly recently, nature and need determined what people ate, and nature was often severe. Most Swedes enjoyed simple, nourishing dishes called *husmanskost*, or traditional home cooking, the comfort food of today—dishes like *sotare*, blackened "chimney sweep" herring with dill; eggy dumplings known as *klimp*; and *klappgröt*, a whipped summer pudding of farina and berries. Of course, those who had money sought out flavors beyond those supported by Sweden's climate. Their desire led to a kind of haute Swedish cuisine based on imported spices and French techniques. This type of cooking flourished in restaurants, especially in Stockholm, thanks largely to the twentieth-century restaurateur Tore Wretman, who had trained in France. Wretman's elegant postwar restaurants Riche and Stallmästaregården (Stablemaster's Farm) gave new definition to Swedish cuisine in their focus on native foods with a French accent. But Wretman never lost his love for Swedish home cooking. In 1967 he published *Svensk husmanskost* (*Swedish Home Cooking*), which applauded the country's ways with whole grains and root vegetables and salted and cured fish, and made them fashionable again.

There's every reason to celebrate *svensk husmanskost*—what Swedish cooks have done so well with so little for so long. Swedish home cooking teases a depth of flavor from just a few basic ingredients to create dishes more spectacular than the sum of their parts. A good example is gravlax, for which fresh salmon is simply rubbed with sugar, white pepper, and salt, covered with dill, and left to cure overnight. The finished dish is lustrous, with complex layers of herb, sweet, salt, and spice. Boiled potatoes can be similarly eye-opening. Knobby fingerlings the size of a man's thumb—what the Swedes call *mandelpotatis*, or "almond potatoes"—are gently boiled, then broken lightly with a fork to reveal their floury, golden flesh. A knob of rich creamery butter, a generous handful of chopped fresh dill, and a sprinkling of sea salt create heaven in a bowl. Though the ingredients are simple, they resonate with a sense of place. These fingerlings were developed in the nineteenth century to thrive in Sweden's north, and while dill is not native to Northern Europe, it became Sweden's defining herbal flavor. The monks who introduced Christianity in the twelfth century probably brought dill to Sweden along with other medicinal and culinary herbs. The word's origin is uncertain, but it's likely that *dill* (in both English and Swedish) derives from the Old Norse *dilla*, which means to calm or to soothe.

For me the smell of fresh dill is less soothing than thrilling, carrying me back, madeleine-like, to my first taste of Sweden. That taste occurred three decades ago, when my husband and I moved as graduate students to Sweden, just weeks after we married. We spent ten months in Stockholm, living in Dickensian penury and newlywed bliss. Our indulgences were few. Every week or so we made our way across Gärdet Field, where the royal sheep still grazed, to an art film at Filmhuset (we once sat next to Anita Ekberg and silently swooned). Just as important for cultural immersion was our weekly visit to Vete-Katten, a café where we lingered over strong Swedish coffee and slices of Princess cake, with mounds of whipped cream draped in pale-green marzipan. Back on the street we would gaze longingly at the menus posted outside the city's great restaurants, but with empty pockets we could only dream of the crayfish, prawns, pike, herring, oysters, cured salmon, and flounder they so enticingly described. That is, until we

befriended Tommy Henriksson, a fishmonger at one of Stockholm's food halls, who took a shine to us and little by little introduced us to the astonishing bounty of Swedish waters. We panfried fresh herring and ate it on crispbread; ground scraps of pike into pâté, and occasionally we splurged on Tommy's exquisite shrimp toast, crowned with tiny, golden vendace roe.

Before we alit in Stockholm, I had little sense of Swedish history and assumed that the Nordic countries had existed only at the periphery of European commerce. In fact, lively trading extends back more than a thousand years in Sweden. The Viking town of Birka, not far from present-day Stockholm, flourished between the eighth and tenth centuries. This wealthy trade center was just one point on a northern "Silk Road" that stretched from Russia to the Middle East, to Constantinople, Jerusalem, and Baghdad. Americans tend to think of the

Vikings as marauding and exploring to the west, but they also ventured far to the south and east, traveling in the ninth century to the Caspian and Black seas, where they traded with Byzantium and the Arab caliphates. They loaded their return ships with coveted textiles and foods and even Mediterranean wines. Salt was imported from the Mediterranean, rye from Russia, spices from Arab lands and China. Wealthy Swedes developed a taste for saffron, cinnamon, and cloves. Beginning in the Middle Ages, a small amount of rice also made its way north. Rice was at first a luxury in Sweden, but once it became more affordable in the late nineteenth century, creamy rice pudding began to replace the coarser porridges of oatmeal and barley, eventually becoming a classic dessert that is still seasoned with cinnamon or saffron.

With the decline of Viking civilization, trade patterns shifted, and the Hanseatic League

became the dominant engine of commerce in the Baltic region. Huge amounts of salt herring, copper, and iron ore moved through the important port of Visby, on the southern island of Gotland, which was ruled by the Danes for three hundred years before returning to Swedish hands in the mid-seventeenth century. By then, Sweden had become a world power, one great enough to have colonial aspirations in the New World. In 1638 the Swedish West India Company founded New Sweden in Delaware, building a fort in what is now Wilmington, and naming it Christina after the Swedish queen (today the community called Christiana is best known for its tax-free shopping mall). The colony lasted until 1655, when it was swallowed up by New Netherland. We have those early Swedish colonists to thank for introducing us to the log cabin, so iconic in American historiography.

Despite its powerful army, Sweden couldn't hold out against the combined forces of Russia, Poland, and Denmark, and its defeat in the Great Northern War meant a loss of much territory and rapid economic decline. Periodic famines beset the struggling populace, and the devastating crop failures of 1867 led to massive migration to the United States. Because grain, largely barley, was in short supply—most was used to produce beer and ale—thin breads (*tunnbröd*) and crispbreads (*knäckebröd*) became widespread, as they required much less grain than yeasted loaves. These flatbreads are still enormously popular, though they're now eaten as an enhancement to fish or cheese, not as an end in themselves. Some of these breads were poverty fare. In a 1796 visit to Sweden, Mary Wollstonecraft, the mother of *Frankenstein*'s creator, encountered hardtack that was "hard enough, you may imagine, as

it is only baked once a year." The reputation of Swedish cuisine has suffered from such bad press over the years.

Because other foodstuffs were so limited, dairy products and dried peas provided important proteins. An astonishing 90 percent of Swedes are lactose tolerant, having adapted early on to rely on dairy. They produced butter and buttermilk and cultured milk into cheese, using the whey to preserve meat and to make whey butter (*messmör*) and whey cheese (*mesost*), whose tangy caramelized flavor is still sought after. Dried yellow peas were made into porridge. Thick pea soup (with smoked bacon or ham for those who could afford it) was eaten on Thursdays, to fill the stomach before Friday's Church-ordained fast. Even today *ärter med fläsk* is a popular Thursday-night supper.

Widespread hunger in the mid-eighteenth century drove Countess Eva Ekeblad De la Gardie to promote the potato. An agronomist and the first woman elected to the Swedish Academy of Sciences, De la Gardie sought to distill alcohol from potatoes so that more grain would be available for bread. She also advocated potato starch for face powder, to replace the arsenic-based powder that women used to whiten their skin. De la Gardie's efforts moved the potato plant out of aristocratic hothouses and into the fields, but it took another century before potatoes were widely cultivated in Sweden.

Hunger was so persistent that the great Swedish taxonomist Carl Linnaeus applied himself to the problem. On a visit to the province of Dalarna he was appalled to find people eating bark bread, made by pulling the bark from trees, drying it, grinding it, and mixing the mass with water. Not only did the bread's lack of nutrients bother him, he also worried about its effect on Sweden's economy, because stripping bark killed the trees necessary for timber export. Linnaeus recommended that people turn to other plant sources like nettles, moss, and bog myrtle—still famine fare, but at least eating them didn't hurt the trees. He also schemed to eliminate the need for expensive imports, believing that warm-weather crops could be cultivated in the inhospitable North by gradually acclimating them to the cold. In his gardens in the university town of Uppsala, just north of Stockholm, Linnaeus planted cacao, rice, cinnamon, tea, sugarcane, ginger, and coffee, among other tropical plants. Not surprisingly, his experiments failed. Nevertheless, he continued to proselytize for the importance of science and reason in a society still living close to the natural world with its unexplained phenomena. In a 1759 speech, he declared that without science, "Demons of the forest would hide in every bush. Specters would haunt every dark corner. Imps, gnomes, river spirits, and the others in Lucifer's gang would live among us like gray cats, and superstition, witchcraft, and black magic would swarm around us like mosquitoes." (Linnaeus may have felt this possibility acutely, as his great-grandmother had been burned as a witch.) His imagery helps us imagine a Sweden very different from the progressive society of today, one in which pagan spirits still threatened mischief; when December's Lucia buns, despite their Christian symbolism, carried connotations of the underworld; when the supernatural gnomes of the past had not yet been transformed into adorable *tomtar*, Christmas elves without ties to the dark spirit world.

These days, of course, Sweden is both modern and prosperous, and stories of the hungry, haunted past tend to sound quaint or outlandish. But Swedes retain a deep affection for forest and bog. This taste for bewitching, intense flavors has been reinvigorated by New Nordic cuisine, in such dishes as toasted oak–infused ice cream, wild mushroom and juniper broth, and meadowsweet mead. Yet even as modernist restaurants proliferate, Swedes cling to certain distinctive ways of taking a meal. First among them is the *smörgåsbord*, originally conceived of as an appetite-whetting prelude to the meal. In the nineteenth century the smorgasbord became more substantial, and by the early twentieth century it had become a lavish meal in itself. When Tore Wretman revived the restaurant Operakällaren (Opera Cellars) in the early 1960s, he amplified the *smörgåsbord* into an event, instituting a protocol that calls for five separate helpings (*turer*, or "tours"), beginning with herring and ending with dessert. The first course, "His Majesty the Herring," offers a parade of pickled, marinated, and cured Atlantic and Baltic herring (*sill* and *strömming*), Swedish anchovies, and sardines; these fish are also mixed into salads, and are presented with crispbreads and cheeses like Västerbotten and Herrgård, respectively tangy and mild. Next comes a second course featuring other types of fish and seafood, including gravlax, boiled shrimp, West Coast seafood salad, smoked whitefish, and mussels; then cold meats, such as smoked reindeer and ham, and others preserved in aspic or made into sausages and pâtés. Various salads and condiments round out this third helping. Then come hot dishes like stuffed cabbage rolls, omelets, and Swedish meatballs, with an array of breads to complement each savory bite. The final dessert course includes fruits, cakes, rice pudding, and tortes like the beloved

Punschtårta, made with chocolate and Punsch, the distinctively Swedish liqueur of rum, arrack, and spices. The spread becomes even more extravagant at Christmas, when restaurants feature a seasonal *Julsmörgåsbord*.

A second distinctive Swedish meal is the *vickning*, a late-night supper also known as *nattamat* ("midnight snack"), often thrown together after a performance or at the end of a long evening at home, to make sure guests are seen off with full bellies—or to mitigate the effect of an evening's worth of schnapps. Contrary to our diet-obsessed proscriptions against eating heavily late at night, this meal calls for the most comforting and calorific of dishes, casseroles like Jansson's Temptation, rich with Swedish anchovies, potatoes, and cream; or the beef and vegetable hash known as *pytt i panna*. There might also be sausages ranging from slightly fermented *isterband*, filled with potatoes and barley, to bite-sized *prinskorv*, served with sweet mustard.

The Swedish meal closest to my heart is the *fika*, whose meaning I came to understand ever so many years ago when my husband and I frequented Stockholm's Vete-Katten. *Fika*—both a noun and a verb in Swedish—approaches a state of being. It means not just the meal, or the act of taking that meal, but the emotion and camaraderie that accompany it. In workplaces throughout the country, *fika* is an institution, a twice-daily break at ten in the morning and again at three. For those not at work, *fika* offers an opportunity to gather at home or in a coffee shop, to catch up on news and enjoy a delicious bite. The meal includes superstrong coffee and *fikabröd,* an abundance of baked goods. Ever since the seventeenth century, when coffee was introduced to Sweden, the Swedes have had a passion for the drink, so much so that coffee imports were banned in the eighteenth century for fear that the beverage would destroy the national health, not to mention the country's morals. In Europe today, the Swedes are second only to the Finns in the amount of coffee they consume annually. Although a *fika* sometimes begins with sandwiches and ends with a selection of *sju sorters kakor* (seven kinds of cookies), it invariably highlights sweet pastries or breads, in offerings that change seasonally. For Fat Tuesday, just before Lent, sinful *semlor* appear, sweet, cardamom-scented buns filled with whipped cream and almond paste. They are so popular that many bakeries now have them on hand from January until March. There might be *mandelkrans*, a wreath of enriched dough filled with almond paste, or *kaffeekringlor*, cardamom-scented twists. *Kanelbullar*, cinnamon buns, are a must. So beloved are these buns that October 4 is National Cinnamon Bun Day.

Today, with nearly one in five Swedes foreign-born, the country's culinary landscape is changing. It is now as easy to find kielbasa and baklava as it is pickled herring. Yet even as society adjusts, the *smörgåsbord, vickning,* and *fika* remain integral to Swedish life as new generations of Swedes embrace them.

SOUPS + PORRIDGE

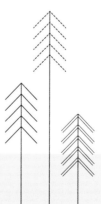

The Nordic kitchen offers soups and porridges for all moods and seasons, from stick-to-the-ribs pea soup in winter—traditionally served each Thursday night—to refreshingly cool fruit soups in summer. Fish soups are common, since they're so easy to prepare from the fresh catch of the day. Root vegetables yield a grab bag of flavors and colors when simmered in broth and pureed.

Scandinavian soups are highly seasonal. In early spring, nettles are foraged to flavor an emerald-green soup rich in vitamins. Summer is celebrated with light broths that highlight the season's first tiny vegetables and with chilled buttermilk soup that gets a lovely pink boost from June's sweet early strawberries. As the days grow long, wild blueberries are gathered by the bucketful, then briefly simmered with cinnamon and lemon before being strained and chilled for a glorious cold bowl. Late summer's chanterelles cook up into a golden, aromatic soup evocative of the forest. Autumn brings warm apple soup scented with juniper. When winter arrives, dried fruits or frozen blueberries are simmered with spices to bring soothing aromas to the house. If Scandinavians need a blast of vitamin C, they can (like the rest of us) pop a pill, but it's so much more sustaining to simmer dried rose hips in water, puree them with a touch of lemon and sugar, and sit down to a bowlful of goodness.

Scandinavians also love porridge. The hardscrabble dish of the past consisted solely of toasted barley flour and water, but in better times, rye, oatmeal, barley, or wheat berries were stirred with water or milk and steamed slowly on the stovetop or baked even more slowly in the oven. *Gröt*, *grød*, and *grøt*—cognates of our English word "gruel," with its harsh, Dickensian associations—convey none of the intense satisfaction that these hearty bowlfuls of grain deliver. Nordic porridges appear at breakfast or supper and sometimes for dessert if they've been cooked with fruit juice or simmered with dried fruits as natural sweeteners. A Nordic Oliver Twist would ask for more gruel not because he's so deprived but because the gruel's so delicious.

IF YOU'VE EVER foraged for mushrooms and suddenly discovered a cache of golden chanterelles, you know what a joy they are to behold. This soup captures that magical moment, even if you haven't gathered the mushrooms yourself. The woodland flavor will come through no matter what, but if you use a flavorful base the soup will really sing. The amount of salt needed will depend on your broth, so be sure to taste before adding any, though a generous grinding of black pepper is always good. If I have enough chanterelles I like to reserve a few and sauté them quickly to garnish each bowlful.

Kanttarellikeitto

# CHANTERELLE SOUP

SERVES 4

1 pound chanterelles

3 tablespoons butter

¼ cup finely chopped yellow onion

¼ cup plus 2 tablespoons finely chopped fresh parsley

2 tablespoons flour

3 cups vegetable broth

½ cup heavy cream

Salt and freshly ground pepper

Pick over the mushrooms and wipe away any forest debris with a damp paper towel. Chop them medium fine.

Melt the butter in a saucepan over medium-low heat and add the mushrooms, onion, and ¼ cup of the parsley. Sauté until the moisture released by the mushrooms evaporates, about 6 minutes. Sprinkle with the flour and stir for a minute more, then gradually whisk in the broth.

Raise the heat to bring to a boil, then lower the heat to simmer for 20 minutes. Stir in the cream, taking care not to let the soup boil. Season with salt and pepper to taste. Stir the remaining 2 tablespoons of parsley into the soup and serve hot.

THIS RECIPE FOR a soul-warming winter soup comes from my dear friend Rachelle Puryear, an artist and translator who moved to Stockholm in 1974. She and her Swedish husband, Håkan, live in a lovely early eighteenth-century building in the city's hip Södermalm district. This is one of Rachelle's favorite soups because it can be put together so easily, with whatever is on hand, and its outcome is always a bit of a surprise. The color can range from golden to garnet, depending on which vegetables you use. The herbs called for here were staples in traditional Swedish kitchen gardens, carefully harvested each autumn and dried for the winter. For a richer flavor, you can use chicken broth, although I love the purely vegetal taste of vegetable broth.

"Man tager vad man haver"

"USE WHAT YOU HAVE" SOUP

SERVES 6

2 tablespoons unsalted butter

6 cups peeled, coarsely chopped root vegetables (such as red or yellow beets, carrots, celery root, parsnips, potatoes, rutabaga, parsley root)

1 large yellow onion, coarsely chopped

2 cloves garlic, coarsely chopped

6 cups vegetable broth

1 cup dry white wine

2 bay leaves

Finely chopped fresh or dried herbs (such as lovage, marjoram, rosemary, and sage)

Salt and freshly ground pepper

½ cup crème fraîche

Melt the butter in a large stockpot over medium-low heat. Add the root vegetables, onion, and garlic, stirring to coat them well in the melted butter. Sauté until the vegetables soften and take on color, about 15 minutes. Stir in the broth, wine, bay leaves, herbs, and ½ teaspoon each salt and pepper. Bring to a boil, then lower the heat and simmer, covered, until the vegetables are very soft, about 1 hour.

Remove the bay leaves and discard. Working in batches, puree the soup in a blender. Return the puree to a clean pot and stir in the crème fraîche. Heat again but don't allow the soup to boil. Season with salt and pepper to taste. Serve hot.

SCANDINAVIANS EAGERLY ANTICIPATE the first nettles poking up aboveground as an early harbinger of spring. The nettles are gathered when still young and are made into a delicate soup with a brilliant green hue. Lacking wild greens, you can make the soup with baby spinach in the spring, or try an autumnal version with kale. Sorrel and potatoes are tasty additions as well. No matter the ingredients, this soup is packed with vitamins.

Nässelsoppa

NETTLE SOUP

SERVES 4

2 tablespoons butter

3 large green onions, coarsely chopped, including the tops

2 tablespoons flour

3 cups chicken stock

12 to 16 ounces fresh nettles or spinach

½ cup plus 2 tablespoons half-and-half

¾ teaspoon salt

Freshly ground white pepper

Freshly grated nutmeg

2 hard-boiled egg yolks, finely chopped

Snipped fresh chives

Melt the butter in a large saucepan over medium heat. Add the green onions, lower the heat to medium-low, and cook until they release their fragrance, a few minutes. Sprinkle with the flour and stir for a minute more, then gradually add the stock, whisking all the while.

Raise the heat to bring to a boil. Add the nettles, lower the heat, and simmer, covered, until the greens are wilted, about 5 minutes.

Working in batches, puree the soup in a blender for a few minutes, until well blended but still retaining some flecks of green. Return the puree to the pot and stir in the half-and-half. Reheat the soup gently over low heat. Stir in the salt and season with pepper and nutmeg to taste.

Garnish with the egg yolks and chives.

THIS AUTUMNAL SOUP captures many of Scandinavia's most essential flavors. The baking spices add a warm, aromatic edge, while the juniper lends a hint of smoke. This soup provides comfort when the first chill nips the air, yet it's elegant enough for a dinner-party first course. Guests rarely guess that apples lie at its heart. I sometimes garnish the soup with finely sliced shallots frizzled in oil until golden.

Eplesuppe med enerbær

 # APPLE SOUP
WITH JUNIPER

SERVES 4 TO 6

2 tablespoons canola oil

1½ pounds tart apples, such as Granny Smith (about 3), peeled and chopped

2 small celery stalks, chopped

2 shallots, chopped

1 (1-inch) piece gingerroot, peeled and finely chopped

1 tablespoon juniper berries

4 cardamom pods

3 allspice berries

1 small cinnamon stick

8 large sprigs parsley

1 sprig thyme

4 cups chicken stock

1 cup apple cider

Salt and freshly ground pepper

Heat the oil in a stockpot over low heat. Toss the apples, celery, shallots, and gingerroot into the pan, then cover and cook gently until they are soft but not brown, 8 to 10 minutes.

Meanwhile, place the juniper, cardamom, allspice, and cinnamon, along with the parsley and thyme, in a piece of cheesecloth and tie it with kitchen twine.

When the apple mixture is softened, pour the chicken stock and cider into the pot. Add the spice and herb bundle and cover the pot. Bring to a boil, then lower the heat and simmer for 40 minutes.

Remove the spice bundle and discard. Working in batches, puree the soup in a blender. Pour the puree through a fine-mesh sieve into a clean pot, pressing down on the solids. Repeat with the remaining soup.

Reheat the soup gently over low heat and season with salt and pepper to taste. Serve hot.

THE SECRET OF this much-loved Finnish soup is good fresh salmon and a good fish stock. With these on hand, it's a snap to prepare, and it comes with a bonus: whoever makes the soup gets to eat the slice of buttered rye bread that has soaked up the stock's goodness. Though you can buy decent fish stock, making your own takes only half an hour, well worth it for the depth of flavor it adds.

Many recipes for *lohikeitto* are heavy with cream. I prefer it on the lighter side and use only 6 tablespoons, but you can certainly do as my husband does and add more, in which case you may need to adjust the salt. I like to make this everyday fare festive by adding a dollop of bright orange trout roe to each bowl.

Lohikeitto

 # SALMON SOUP

SERVES 4 TO 6

SALMON STOCK

1 salmon head (about 3 pounds), cleaned, with gills removed

1 small yellow onion, halved

1 carrot, peeled and halved

1 bay leaf

8 black peppercorns

1 teaspoon salt

8 cups water

SOUP

1 yellow onion, finely chopped

1 tablespoon salted butter

4 boiling potatoes, peeled and cut into ¾-inch cubes

Pinch of ground allspice

6 cups Salmon Stock (see recipe) or prepared fish stock

Salt

Freshly ground pepper

1 thick slice sour rye bread, liberally buttered on one side

1 pound salmon fillet, skin removed, cut into 1-inch pieces

6 to 8 tablespoons heavy cream

¼ cup finely chopped fresh dill

1 (2-ounce) jar trout roe

Place the salmon head, onion, carrot, bay leaf, peppercorns, and salt in a large stockpot. Add the water and bring to a boil. Lower the heat and simmer, partly covered, for 30 minutes. Strain with a fine-mesh sieve into a large Pyrex measuring cup and set aside. Discard the salmon head and other solids.

In a large stockpot over medium-low heat, sauté the onion in the butter until soft but not brown, 6 to 7 minutes.

Add the potatoes and allspice, then stir in the stock and ¾ teaspoon of salt. Season with pepper. Place the bread on the surface of the stock, buttered side up, and cover the pot. Simmer until the potatoes are just cooked, about 10 minutes.

With a slotted spatula, remove the bread (and eat it!). At this point you can either continue making the soup or turn off the heat and let it sit until you're almost ready to serve it. About 10 minutes before serving, return the soup to a simmer. Drop in the salmon and cook very briefly, until the fish is barely opaque, just 3 to 4 minutes.

Quickly stir in the cream and dill, making sure not to let the soup boil. Taste and add liberal grinds of pepper and more salt to taste. To serve, ladle into bowls and garnish each serving with a spoonful of trout roe.

SUMMER SOUP CAN polarize a party of Finns. For some it's the stuff of bad childhood memories, a bland soup with limp vegetables that were stored too long, their tired flavors masked by cream. But if Summer Soup is made the way it should be—with the sweetest vegetables of early summer—it's a thing of beauty, refreshing and celebratory.

Part of Summer Soup's appeal is its flexibility. Just about anything that looks its best in the garden can be included. This recipe, from the talented chef Nick Victorzon, calls for carrots, potatoes, asparagus, peas, cauliflower, and green onions. You could also add baby turnips or radishes. Most versions call for more milk, even light cream, in proportion to water, but Nick's rendition makes for a lighter, fresh-tasting soup. For a luxurious finish he adds an egg yolk and beurre manié.

Kesäkeitto

 SUMMER SOUP

SERVES 6

2 cups water

1½ teaspoons salt

6 new potatoes

3 small carrots

2 cups cauliflower florets

1 cup asparagus tips (flowered tops only) or sliced green beans

1 cup freshly shelled peas (from around 1 pound of peas in the pod)

2 or 3 green onions, thinly sliced

2 cups whole milk

4 tablespoons flour

2 tablespoons butter, at room temperature

1 egg yolk

½ cup fresh spinach, stemmed and cut into strips

¼ cup chopped fresh parsley

Freshly ground white pepper to taste

1 teaspoon sugar (optional, depending on how sweet the vegetables are)

Bring the water and salt to a boil in a stockpot. Scrub the potatoes and carrots but don't peel them unless the skins are tough. Drop the potatoes and carrots into the water and cook them for 5 minutes. Stir in the cauliflower, asparagus, peas, green onions and return to a gentle boil.

Meanwhile, in a bowl, gradually whisk the milk into 2 tablespoons of the flour until there are no lumps, then stir the mixture into the soup. Simmer the soup about 8 minutes more, until the broth thickens slightly and the vegetables are just done—they should be tender but still slightly crisp.

With your fingers, mix together the butter and the remaining 2 tablespoons of the flour in a bowl. Stir in the egg yolk. Whisk this enriched beurre manié into the soup and simmer gently until the soup thickens slightly, 1 to 2 minutes more.

Stir in the spinach and parsley and season to taste with white pepper. Add a little sugar if needed. Serve hot.

THIS EASY, REFRESHING soup captures the intensity of summer's ripe berries. The amount of sugar you use will depend on how tart your berries are, so add a little at a time and keep tasting before removing the soup from the heat. It is not meant to be especially sweet. Cold fruit soups like this can be served for lunch or as a light dessert. In Finland they sometimes even appear at breakfast.

Kold blåbær suppe

CHILLED BLUEBERRY SOUP

SERVES 4 TO 6

4 cups water

4 cups fresh blueberries

5 tablespoons sugar (or to taste)

½ small lemon, sliced

1 small cinnamon stick

Place the water, blueberries, sugar, lemon, and cinnamon in a medium saucepan. Bring to a boil, then lower the heat and simmer until the blueberries soften, 5 to 7 minutes. Remove the lemon and cinnamon , then strain the blueberry mixture into a bowl, pressing down on the pulp to extract as much liquid as possible. Discard the lemon, cinnamon, and blueberry pulp. Let the soup cool to room temperature and then refrigerate, covered, for at least 2 hours. Serve chilled.

VARIATION: During winter, use frozen blueberries and serve the soup hot. Don't thaw the berries before cooking.

LONG BEFORE SMOOTHIES became an international phenomenon, the Danes were enjoying buttermilk soup–a smoothie in a bowl. This classic dessert is enriched with egg yolks, or sometimes *fromage frais*. I substitute Greek-style yogurt and add some strawberries for color. To make the dish even prettier, freeze a few small whole berries and drop them into the soup at the last minute to give it a chilly boost on a hot summer's day. Danes often garnish the soup with tiny sugar cookies.

I prefer this soup tart, as the Danes do, but if you want to mellow the tang, you can add some confectioners' sugar or a little Rhubarb Refresher (page 279). Because the soup's deliciousness depends on rich, flavorful buttermilk, seek out the best buttermilk you can find.

Kærnemælks koldskål

BUTTERMILK SOUP
WITH STRAWBERRIES

SERVES 4

1 cup fresh strawberries

2 cups organic buttermilk

2 cups Greek-style yogurt
(I use 2% fat)

1 teaspoon lemon zest

Confectioners' sugar or
Rhubarb Refresher (page 279),
for sweetening (optional)

Put the strawberries, buttermilk, yogurt, and lemon zest in a blender and puree. If desired, the soup can be sweetened with sugar or rhubarb refresher to taste. Refrigerate for at least 1 hour, and up to 2 days. Serve chilled.

FINLAND IS THE land of porridge, made in dozens of varieties from different grains. Traditionally served for supper or dessert, it is now found at breakfast. When my husband and I stayed at the elegant Tertti Manor in Mikkeli, we were told we mustn't leave without tasting their special porridge. I'm so glad we obeyed.

The world is divided into two kinds of people, those who love porridge and those who think they can't stand it. If, like me, you are a porridge lover, you'll enjoy this recipe, for which cracked rye is cooked slowly overnight to yield an ultra-creamy porridge ready for breakfast. Because dried berries lend natural sweetness, no additional sweetening is needed. Serve the porridge with hot milk or cold cream, and perhaps a sprinkling of cinnamon. Any leftovers can be spread in a greased pan and chilled overnight. Slice and fry the cold porridge in a little butter, as you would polenta, and serve with a spoonful of jam.

Ruisuunipuuro

OVEN RYE PORRIDGE

SERVES 4

Butter for greasing the baking dish

1 cup cracked rye

¾ to 1 cup dried cranberries or blueberries

¼ teaspoon salt

3 cups boiling water

Preheat the oven to 250°F. Butter an ovenproof 2-quart casserole—I like to use a ceramic bean pot. Stir together the cracked rye, cranberries, and salt in the pot, then pour the boiling water over the top. Give everything a good stir, cover, and place the pot in the oven. Lower the heat to 200°F and cook the porridge until the water has been absorbed and the grains are tender but still chewy, about 8 hours. Serve as soon as it's removed from the oven.

foraging

THE MOSSY PINE forests of the North hold many treasures. Golden chanterelles hide among pine needles; cèpes rise up near the roots of the trees. Nearly one hundred types of edible mushrooms grow in the North, and half as many different berries, all there for the taking. The principle of common good is important to the Scandinavian ethos. Sweden, Norway, and Finland all adhere to "everyman's right," the freedom to roam through forest and field and forage for wild plants, as long you're not destructive. Originally designed to foster self-sufficiency, these rights now encourage a joyous pastime that helps define seasonal rhythms.

Spring offers up vivid green shoots of spruce and pine, along with tiny birch leaves and birch sap, all packed with vitamins that are particularly welcome after snow-covered months. These gifts from the trees flavor beverages, from citrusy sparklers to heavy-duty schnapps. Spruce shoots can be stirred into salt or infused in oil to bring a hint of the forest to any meal, or they can be mixed with sugar or syrup to enliven desserts. The pungent young leaves of lady's mantle add depth to salads, while the tender stalks of fireweed, harvested before the plants burst into magenta bloom, can be steamed like asparagus. In Finland, black currant leaves are fermented with sugar, water, lemon, and a little yeast into a bubbly drink. They also lend a subtle herbal note to brined meat and cucumbers. Scandinavia's towering angelica plants, rising up to ten feet, provide much more than just candied decoration. The Sami treat the young stalks as a vegetable, munching them crisp and raw like celery, or charring them over flames. The roasted seeds are a lively fennel substitute. Other foraged plants include mountain, wood, and sheep's sorrel, which are cooked up into spinach-like soups or tart sauces for fish. Meadowsweet blossoms yield a beautiful, pale yellow cordial, and both blossoms and leaves make a comforting tisane. Meadowsweet's assuaging properties, coupled with its botanical name of *Spirea ulmaria*, gave rise to the nineteenth-century synthesis and trade name of Aspirin.

Nordic summers usher in a parade of berries. First to ripen are tiny wild strawberries that children thread onto stalks of grass and then shape into wreaths for their heads to celebrate the season. Where timber has been cut, thickets of wild raspberries abound. Even sweeter is the wild raspberry's cousin, the arctic bramble, which grows in damp meadows and swamps. Golden cloudberries ripen in August in the northern bogs, a favorite habitat of mosquitoes. Along back roads and byways it's common to encounter foragers emerging from the muck, swathed head to toe in protective gear, intent on reaching their cars as quickly as possible, pursued by clouds of mosquitoes. This ritual is repeated throughout the berries' brief season, since their exquisite taste is worth any amount of itching. Even when frozen, cloudberries lose little of their musky charm, and they appear on the table throughout the winter like so many rays of sunshine. August also brings bilberries, crowberries, and blueberries, which—if you can resist gobbling them all before getting home—fill an array of pies, tarts, puddings, and soups, and are pressed into an antioxidant-rich drink. Early September dazzles with lingonberries. These late-season berries contain so much natural benzoic acid that they can be kept in water for months, or stirred simply with sugar to avoid losing vitamins from cooking. No wonder they're considered the "red gold" of the North.

SALADS

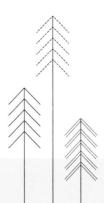

Salads in Scandinavia are so much more than mixed greens. In the past, the cold temperatures of the North meant that only the aristocracy could enjoy vegetables like lettuce, which they planted alongside other delicacies in their showcase gardens. The rest of the population had to make do with heartier tubers and roots, but they used them inventively, especially in composed salads. It's easy enough now to buy lettuce in grocery stores throughout Scandinavia, but that tender leaf seems pallid when compared to Nordic ingredients that offer an earthier taste of place.

Why not try using thinly sliced cauliflower instead of cabbage when you're in the mood for brassicas? Mixed with red onions and radishes, this vitamin-rich salad brings beautiful color to the winter table, as do salads of other sturdy vegetables like celery root and beets. All of the Nordic countries make versions of dilled sweet-and-sour cucumbers with varying degrees of vinegary kick. More unusual is the pairing of cucumbers with refreshingly tart rhubarb, which gets to escape from its usual sugared treatment to appear as the vegetable it is. Diced beets turn mundane potato salad rosy while apples lend a fruity note. Barley needn't be relegated only to porridge or bread. It becomes a sprightly salad when stirred with plenty of herbs.

The most glorious Nordic salads are those made with seafood. Salmon fresh or smoked is often paired with new potatoes in summer. Smoked herring or mackerel can be chopped with cucumbers, red onions, and capers and served on slices of rye or mounded on lettuce. Sweet, tiny bay shrimp are dressed with a light vinaigrette to accompany a jelled puree of vivid green asparagus so delicious that it will turn your notion of congealed salads on end. West Coast Salad (see page 113), abundant with shrimp, mussels, and crabmeat, is a showstopper, especially when offered with a duo of sauces, a dill vinaigrette and the intriguingly named Rhode Island sauce, a type of Thousand Island dressing.

THESE QUICK-PICKLED CUCUMBERS are a summer staple in Finland. The recipe below, courtesy of Maria Planting, is to my mind perfect—vivacious and less acidic than the Hungarian-style cucumbers I always used to make. I suppose I'm also charmed by the name of this salad, which translates to something like "shaken not stirred cucumbers." I call them "swished." The traditional way of making them calls for putting the sliced cucumbers and their dressing in a pot with a lid, and vigorously shaking it back and forth until they give off their liquid. Finnish arms must be stronger than mine, or temperaments different, because I don't have the patience to make them in the time-honored way. Neither does Maria, so she shared her trick as well as her recipe for making this lovely accompaniment to warm smoked fish and cold sliced meat.

Hölskykurkut

 SWISHED CUCUMBERS

SERVES 4

1 pound cucumber (about 1 English cucumber)

½ cup chopped fresh dill

3 tablespoons distilled white vinegar

2 tablespoons sugar

1 teaspoon salt

If the cucumber has a tough skin, peel it; otherwise there's no need to. Slice the cucumber thinly and place the slices in a bowl. Mix together the dill, vinegar, sugar, and salt in another bowl, pour over the cucumber, and stir to combine. Place a small nonreactive plate over the cucumber mixture, then set a heavy can or other weight on top of the plate to press the cucumbers slightly. Refrigerate the cucumbers with the weight, allowing the flavors to develop for 2 to 3 hours.

When ready to serve, lift the cucumbers out of the liquid with a slotted spoon. Serve chilled.

THIS VIVID PINK salad is a fixture on the Finnish Christmas table. While similar salads appear in Estonia and Russia—the name, in fact, comes from the Russian root for "pickle"—I prefer this Finnish version for its lightness. The proportion of beets to potatoes is higher, and sweet cream rather than heavier sour cream serves as the binding agent. Although the brine from pickled beets makes the salad exceptionally colorful, you can substitute dill pickle brine in a pinch. Even though boiling and dicing so many vegetables may seem arduous, it's not once you get organized. This salad can be held in the refrigerator for a couple of days, awaiting dressing and guests.

Rosolli

POTATO SALAD
WITH APPLES AND BEETS
SERVES 8 TO 10

2 potatoes, such as russet

3 beets

2 large carrots, peeled

1 large tart apple, such as Granny Smith, diced

4 baby dill pickles, diced

1 large shallot, finely chopped

1 teaspoon salt

Freshly ground white pepper

1 cup heavy cream

1 tablespoon pickled beet brine or dill pickle brine

Place the potatoes in a large pot of cold salted water and bring to a boil, cooking until tender but firm, about 25 minutes—be careful not to overcook them. Drain, and when cool enough to handle, peel and dice them. Transfer the potatoes to a large bowl.

In a separate pot, boil the beets in salted water until just tender, 35 to 40 minutes. Drain, and when cool enough to handle, peel and dice them. Add the beets to the bowl with the potatoes.

In yet another pot, boil the carrots in salted water until just tender, about 25 minutes. Drain, dice, and add to the bowl with the potatoes and beets.

Stir in the apple, pickles, shallot, and salt. Season with pepper, and mix everything together well. Cover and refrigerate at least overnight and for up to two days in the refrigerator.

Just before serving, lightly whip the cream with a mixer on high speed or by hand until it forms soft peaks. Fold in the pickled beet brine. Spoon the cream mixture over the salad. *Rosolli* can be served straight from the refrigerator, but it tastes even better when the vegetables are allowed to sit at room temperature for an hour or so before dressing them.

VARIATIONS: For a more robust salad, you can substitute diced pickled beets for some or all of the boiled beets. You can also add some chopped pickled herring.

THIS DANISH SALAD is an antidote to winter—bright, crisp, and filled with vitamins. The Danes use rapeseed (canola) oil for most of their cooking, but I like to add a little olive oil to enhance the salad's fruity notes. Good cider vinegar is also a must—make sure you don't use one that is simply "cider flavored." Although dicing the vegetables by hand may seem a little tedious in this era of the food processor, it only takes a few minutes and yields a better texture. The small size of the chunks allows the salad to cohere. Feel free to play around with the proportions of vegetables.

Salat af rå tern

 # CHOPPED WINTER SALAD

SERVES 4

1 large tart apple, such as Granny Smith (8 ounces), diced

6 ounces celery root, peeled and diced

1 small red or yellow beet (about 3 ounces), peeled and diced

4 teaspoons cider vinegar

1½ teaspoons Dijon mustard

1 small clove garlic, minced

¼ teaspoon salt

Freshly ground pepper

2 tablespoons canola oil

2 tablespoons olive oil

1 to 2 tablespoons minced fresh parsley

1 to 2 tablespoons minced fresh dill

Stir together the apple, celery root, and beet in a bowl.

In another bowl, stir together the vinegar, mustard, garlic, and salt. Season with pepper, then gradually whisk in the oils until an emulsion forms.

Pour the dressing over the vegetables and stir in parsley and dill to taste until everything is well combined, and the salad is ready to serve.

BARLEY IS ONE of the oldest cultivated grains, and Nordic cuisine is unthinkable without it. The milled flour goes into all sorts of pancakes and breads, and the world would certainly be a poorer place without barley malted ale! Here the whole grain is cooked into a healthy salad with an appealingly nutty taste. If you like a chewy texture, as I do, be sure to use hulled barley, not pearled, which has had the bran removed. Hulled barley has to be soaked overnight, and it takes longer to cook, but it delivers deeply satisfying flavor along with its nutrients. Feel free to play around with the herbs according to your own taste, since they'll largely define the salad's profile. Or try substituting spelt berries for the barley.

Byggrynssalat

BARLEY SALAD

SERVES 4

4 ounces (¾ cup) hulled barley

6 cups water

2½ teaspoons salt

2 tablespoons canola oil

1 tablespoon cider vinegar

Freshly ground pepper

2 tablespoons finely chopped fresh parsley

2 tablespoons snipped fresh chives

2 tablespoons finely chopped fresh chervil

3 green onions, thinly sliced, including the tops

Soak the barley overnight in cold water to cover. The next day, rinse and drain it.

In a large pot, bring the 6 cups of water and 2 teaspoons of salt to a boil. Add the soaked barley and cook, covered, over medium heat until the grains are softened but still chewy, about 35 minutes. Drain and transfer to a bowl.

Whisk together the oil, vinegar, and remaining ½ teaspoon of salt in another bowl. Season with pepper. While the barley is still warm, stir in the parsley, chives, chervil, and green onions. Pour the dressing over the barley mixture and stir until the barley is well coated. Let the salad sit for an hour at room temperature. Serve at room temperature or chilled.

NORWAY GROWS AMAZING cauliflower, and this crisp, colorful salad is a good way to feature it, packed as it is with vitamins. The salad is a fine choice for picnics because it holds well, and the flavor improves on standing.

Blomkålsalat med reddik

CAULIFLOWER AND RADISH SALAD

SERVES 8

2 pounds cauliflower
(about 1 small)

1 small red onion

3 large radishes

½ cup finely chopped fresh parsley

DRESSING

¼ cup cider vinegar

1½ teaspoons Dijon mustard

¾ cup canola oil

½ teaspoon salt

Freshly ground white pepper

2 tablespoons minced fresh chives

Core the cauliflower and separate it into small florets. Thinly slice the stems. Place the florets and sliced stems in a large bowl.

Peel the onion and slice it very thinly, then cut the slices in half to form half-moons. Trim the radishes and slice them very thinly too. If they are especially large, cut them in half, as you did with the onion. Add the onion and radishes to the cauliflower, then stir in the parsley.

To make the dressing, stir together the vinegar and mustard in a small bowl. Gradually whisk in the oil until an emulsion forms. Add the salt and season with white pepper to taste. You should have about 1 cup of dressing.

Toss about ¾ cup of the dressing with the vegetables, adding more if you want the salad to be tangier. Save any remaining dressing for another use. Let the salad sit at room temperature for several hours to allow the flavors to blend.

Before serving, garnish with the chives and sprinkle with more salt and a few grindings of white pepper to taste. Serve at room temperature, and store any leftovers in the refrigerator.

THIS RECIPE COMES from my neighbor Jytte Brooks, a native of Denmark who first came to the States many years ago as an exchange student. She started out at New Haven's Gesell Institute of Child Development but her interests eventually led her to the creative arts—cooking among them. She ran a popular summer café at the Clark Art Institute for many years.

Jytte makes her summer terrine with green beans, asparagus, or a mix of the two. I like it with just asparagus, for the deeper flavor. I also use less gelatin for a softer consistency. Light and refreshing, this dish makes an elegant summer luncheon, especially if you prepare the terrine in an old-fashioned ring mold and pile the shrimp salad in the center. But any mold will do, even a square cake pan. Simply slice the terrine instead of inverting it and plate it with some shrimp salad on the side.

The terrine must be prepared a day ahead of time. But if you don't feel like going to the trouble of making a terrine, the shrimp salad is excellent on its own or, with a little lettuce, as a topping for an open-faced sandwich.

Rejesalat med dill-og asparges terrine

SHRIMP SALAD
WITH ASPARAGUS-DILL TERRINE

SERVES 8

1 pound cooked bay shrimp (about 2 cups)

2 small celery stalks, minced

4 green onions, minced

1 tablespoon Dijon mustard

1 tablespoon honey

1 tablespoon white wine vinegar

¼ cup canola oil

Pinch of salt

Freshly ground pepper

Asparagus-Dill Terrine (see recipe, page 110)

In a large bowl, stir together the shrimp, celery, and green onions.

To make the dressing, stir together the mustard, honey, and vinegar in a small bowl. Gradually whisk in the oil until an emulsion forms. Stir in the salt and season with pepper to taste.

Pour the dressing over the shrimp mixture and stir until everything is well combined. Refrigerate for at least 1 hour before serving.

To serve the salad, unmold the terrine. Fill a bowl wide enough to hold the mold with hot water. Run a blunt knife around the edges of the mold, then dip the bottom in the hot water for about 30 seconds, to loosen the terrine. Place a serving platter over the top of the mold and invert the terrine onto it. Fill the center with shrimp salad.

CONTINUED

SHRIMP SALAD WITH ASPARAGUS-DILL TERRINE
CONTINUED

ASPARAGUS-DILL TERRINE

1½ pounds asparagus

1 cup water

1 cup lightly packed fresh dill, coarse stems removed

1 envelope (1 tablespoon) unflavored gelatin

2 tablespoons vegetable bouillon

1 cup heavy cream

1 teaspoon salt

¼ teaspoon freshly ground white pepper

To make the terrine, trim the woody ends off the asparagus spears and cut the spears in half crosswise. You should have about 1 pound of asparagus. Place the asparagus in a large skillet with the water over medium-low heat. Cook, covered, until tender, about 5 minutes, depending on the thickness of the spears. With a slotted spoon, transfer the asparagus to the bowl of a food processor, reserving the cooking water.

Add the dill to the food processor and whir into a fine puree.

In a bowl, soften the gelatin in the bouillon, then whisk in the reserved cooking water until the gelatin dissolves. (If the gelatin doesn't dissolve, heat the mixture gently over low heat.) Whisk in the asparagus puree, cream, salt, and pepper.

Rinse a 1-quart mold (ideally one with a hole in the center) with cold water. Pour in the asparagus mixture, smoothing the top. Cover lightly with plastic wrap and refrigerate overnight.

THIS ZESTY SALAD has an evolving personality. When newly made, it is lightly spiced and refreshing. The longer it ages, the more it resembles a condiment, a vinegary counterpoint to rich meats. The salad's fruitiness comes not only from rhubarb but also from pink peppercorns, which are actually berries of an evergreen native to South America. This is a great summer salad. And yet, even though rhubarb isn't seasonal in winter, I can't help associating this dish with Christmas, due to the beautiful pink peppercorns I bought at Copenhagen's Tivoli Christmas market after happening upon a wonderland of organic spices among all the fairy lights.

Rabarber og agurkesalat

FRESH RHUBARB AND CUCUMBER SALAD

SERVES 4 TO 6

8 ounces rhubarb, trimmed

1 English cucumber, peeled

½ cup cider vinegar

½ cup water

2 tablespoons sugar

1 tablespoon cracked pink peppercorns

1 teaspoon salt

1 (1-inch) piece gingerroot, peeled and grated

With the slicing blade of a food processor or a sharp knife, cut the rhubarb and cucumber into ⅛-inch slices. Transfer the rhubarb and cucumber to a medium bowl.

In a saucepan, bring the vinegar, water, sugar, pink peppercorns, and salt to a boil. Lower the heat and simmer until the sugar and salt have dissolved, 2 to 3 minutes, then stir in the ginger. Immediately pour the hot brine over the rhubarb-cucumber mixture.

Cover the bowl with plastic wrap and allow the salad to cool to room temperature, at which point it will be ready to serve. Alternatively, transfer it to the refrigerator, where it will keep for several days.

WEST COAST SALAD showcases the stunning bounty of the sea. Its classic ingredients are shrimp, mussels, crabmeat, and mushrooms, but lobster tails are often included. The vegetables can vary, too, with peas sometimes replacing asparagus. Some cooks add hard-boiled eggs to the salad, either mixed in or as a garnish, and summer-ripe tomatoes can also appear. The only constant, and crucial, element is the freshness of the ingredients. When the salad has a balance of sweetness and brininess, it really sings.

This recipe calls for some attention to its many different steps, but each one is simple. Once cooked, the components can be refrigerated and then assembled in a jiffy, making this an entertainment-easy summer meal. Opinions differ on how best to present the salad, whether on a platter with the ingredients laid out like a mosaic, or layered in a bowl. I generally use a glass bowl to show off the layers, then toss them gently with vinaigrette at the table. The second dressing may at first seem like overkill, but it makes the salad even more festive.

The Swedes call the second tomato-mayonnaise dressing "Rhode Island sauce." Some sources say that the great restaurateur Tore Wretman named it; others credit Werner Vögeli, the vaunted chef at Stockholm's Operakällaren. Exactly where the name comes from remains a mystery. Perhaps, like our Thousand Island dressing, it's a nod to a region similarly known for its seafood.

Vestkystsalat

 WEST COAST SALAD

SERVES 6 TO 8

8 ounces small white mushrooms

1 tablespoon freshly squeezed lemon juice

2 cups water

1 cup dry white wine

1 tablespoon salt

1 pound unpeeled small or medium shrimp

1 pound mussels, cleaned

8 ounces fresh crabmeat

1 pound asparagus

2 heads Bibb lettuce

Garlic-Dill Vinaigrette (see recipe, page 114)

Creamy Dressing (see recipe, page 114)

Trim the mushrooms and cut into ¼-inch slices. Toss with the lemon juice in a bowl and set aside in the refrigerator.

In a large pot, bring the water, ½ cup of the wine, and salt to a boil. Ideally, you're using small shrimp (51/60 count per pound), so cook them for just over a minute. If using medium shrimp, adjust the cooking time accordingly—they need to cook about 2 minutes before they are done. Drain the shrimp, and when they are cool enough to handle, peel and devein them. If using medium shrimp, slice them in half lengthwise to make them bite-size. Set aside, covered, in the refrigerator.

Place the mussels in a large pot with the remaining ½ cup of wine. Cover the pot, bring to a boil over medium-high heat, and

CONTINUED

WEST COAST SALAD
CONTINUED

GARLIC-DILL VINAIGRETTE

¼ cup white wine vinegar

1½ teaspoons Dijon mustard

2 cloves garlic, minced

¾ cup canola oil

½ teaspoon salt

Freshly ground pepper

½ cup chopped fresh dill

CREAMY DRESSING

½ cup crème fraîche

½ cup mayonnaise

1 tablespoon concentrated tomato paste

¼ teaspoon salt

Freshly ground pepper

cook until the mussels open wide, 5 to 7 minutes, depending on their size. Turn off the heat and discard any mussels that didn't open. Drain, discarding the cooking liquid. When cool enough to handle, remove the mussels from their shells. You should have about 4 ounces of mussels. Set aside, covered, in the refrigerator.

Trim the woody ends off the asparagus spears and cut the spears into thirds crosswise. Bring a little salted water to a boil in a skillet and add the asparagus. Lower to medium-low heat and cook, covered, until just tender but still crisp, 3 to 4 minutes. Drain and immediately run under cold water to stop the cooking. Set aside, covered, in the refrigerator.

Wash the lettuce and discard any blemished outer leaves. Tear into bite-size pieces. You should have about 6 loosely packed cups of lettuce.

To make the vinaigrette, stir together the vinegar, mustard, and garlic in a small bowl. Gradually whisk in the oil until an emulsion forms. Add the salt and season with pepper to taste, then stir in the dill.

To make the creamy dressing, stir together all of the ingredients in a small bowl. Set aside in the refrigerator.

To assemble the salad, decoratively arrange the prepared mushrooms, shrimp, mussels, crabmeat, asparagus, and lettuce on a large platter or layer them in a shallow bowl. Just before serving, pour half of the vinaigrette over the ingredients, passing the remaining vinaigrette in a small pitcher at the table. Serve with the creamy dressing in a bowl on the side.

DENMARK

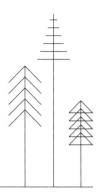

Hamlet might have been a comedy if Shakespeare had encountered *hygge*, a transformative idea that turns bleakness into beauty, gloom into gaiety. *Hygge* encompasses notions of coziness and conviviality, defenses against darkness and the wintertime blues. It's a state of mind created by warmth, friendship, and light, as when friends share a bowl of *gløgg* in front of a fire or pints of crisp beer while candles cast shadows, softening the darkness. *Hygge* goes back to the Old Norse *huggan*, which meant "comfort" or "consolation." And what better source of comfort than a hug, a word *huggan* also spawned? The Norsemen knew that human contact is the best antidote for the blues, especially when it's amplified with a good brew.

Brewing is an ancient practice in Denmark, dating back to around 1370 BCE. Early beers were sweetened with honey and flavored with local plants and natural products like bog myrtle, cranberries, and pollen. Hops were introduced only in the Middle Ages, with the spread of Christian monasteries and their traditions of brewing and distilling. The Danes eventually took a liking to pale lagers, and for many years their beer making was standardized and unchanging. But no longer. On the island of Fanø, off Denmark's west coast, they've experimented with invasive Pacific oysters to make oyster stout. Like some other brewers of oyster stout, they boiled whole oysters with the beer so that the calcium in their shells would help clarify it. Standard practice is to toss the beer-infused bivalves, but on Fanø Island, they fished them out for a savory snack.

Such innovation seems unsurprising in Denmark, the epicenter of New Nordic cuisine, but until the seismic rise of Copenhagen's restaurant Noma, Denmark's culinary traditions tended toward the conservative. This cautious approach had much to do with the country's geography. Denmark consists of more than four hundred low-lying islands left from glacial deposits of gravel, sand, and clay, a landscape the Danes call "flat as a dinner plate." Many bogs provided peat for fuel, but they were unsuitable for agriculture. To create arable land the native forests were progressively destroyed, until by the beginning of the nineteenth century less than 3 percent of the country remained wooded.

Once wood was scarce, salting, rather than smoking, became the main method for preserving meat and fish, especially the herring that was one of Denmark's great exports. Along the coasts, salt marshes predominated, but the climate wasn't warm or sunny enough to evaporate salt. Early Danes burned dune grass to extract salt from the plants, but this practice caused terrible erosion. Other methods proved just as costly to the environment. Because the island of Læsø off the northeast coast of Jutland had exceptionally salty groundwater and was also forested, a great salt industry developed there in the Middle Ages. The water was concentrated in the island's meadows and then boiled in special kilns over wood fires to crystallize the salt. This process produced excellent sea salt but required huge amounts of fuel, and by the mid-seventeenth century the island was deforested. What had once been known as the feasting place of the Norse gods became a desert, and the saltworks shut down. (Læsø was eventually reforested in the early twentieth century.)

Human industriousness changed the landscape in other ways too. Denmark today has some of the most productive soil in Europe, but it didn't start out that way. The country's soil was thin, covering an underlayer of limestone. The difficult growing conditions produced wonderfully flavorful grains, particularly the malting barley used in brewing beer, but inhibited successful cultivation of vegetables. Centuries of growing grain improved the soil incrementally, but only in the mid-nineteenth century did a great leap occur, thanks to reforms in agricultural legislation that encouraged smallholder farms. These small-scale farmers began to raise poultry and pigs, whose manure enriched the poor soil. (None other than the industrialist and philanthropist Andrew Carnegie applauded the new legislation and the rise of agricultural cooperatives, which he saw as a means of promoting equitability and democracy.) The first cooperative dairy was established in 1882, and cooperatives are still going strong today, especially in pork and dairy production. Unusually for a modern European nation, Denmark remained largely agrarian until the late 1950s. The country is still renowned for its cultured butter, flavored by grasses from rich pastureland reclaimed from the sea and enhanced with a touch of sea salt.

The success of the pork and dairy cooperatives encouraged a diet based on meat and dairy (the Danish love of pork is evident in the large number of *pølse*–hot dog–stands punctuating the landscape). But the Danish trinity of roast pork, potatoes, and cabbage required more than animal husbandry. Even more land was needed for cultivating crops. So the Danes drained bogs and dammed fjords to create farmland with soil uncommonly rich in organic matter. The most ambitious project took place in Lammefjord, once a shallow fjord in northwest Zealand, the country's main island. Draining was carried out for seventy years, from 1873 to 1943. This reclaimed seabed lies twenty-three feet below sea level and enjoys an astonishing sixty-six-foot layer of silt. Its exceptional soil nourishes vegetables so extraordinary in taste (especially carrots and radishes) that Noma and other fine restaurants feature them on their menus.

Vegetables and fruits are important to the traditional Danish table, and they mitigate the richness of meat and dairy. Piquant pickled beets, sweet-and-sour cucumbers, red cabbage braised with tart apples and black currant juice, all serve as counterpoints. A tangy contrast is also provided in refreshing desserts like cold buttermilk soup and Denmark's famous *rødgrød*, a red currant, strawberry, and raspberry pudding. Fruits are frequently intensified with spices. Gooseberry jam gets pizzazz from mustard seed, rhubarb from ginger and cardamom. Rose hips boil up with clove and ginger into aromatic chutney, while dried fruits are simmered with cinnamon and allspice into a cheering winter soup. And in a New Nordic vitamin blast, carrots are pressed into juice with apples and rowanberries.

Although Denmark is one of the world's oldest and once most powerful monarchies (the Danish king Canute ruled over England, Norway, and southern Sweden), Danish cuisine shows less influence from royal kitchens than might be expected. Instead, Danish food reflects a long farming tradition marked by simplicity, a practical approach also visible in midcentury Danish modern design. Whether in kitchen or studio, the Danes think about functionalism and truth to materials—or ingredients. But that doesn't mean a lack of aesthetics. Color, texture, and compatibility of components are all-important. In design, Denmark gave the world Nanna Ditzel's hanging egg chair and Arne Jacobsen's stylish flatware (seen in *2001: A Space Odyssey*). In the kitchen, we find *æbleflæsk*, streaky bacon with diced apples whose tartness cuts the meat's richness and provides contrasting texture; and *flæskesteg med rotmos*, roast pork with rutabaga, in which the earthy, golden rutabaga both brightens the plate and heightens the flavor of the pork.

Traditional culinary design reached its heights in *smørrebrød*, the artistically composed open-faced sandwiches that celebrate Denmark's quintessential flavors. So critical are craftsmanship and artistry to the success of the *smørrebrød* that years of training and apprenticeship are required for certification as a *smørrebrødsjomfru*

or "sandwich maid," which despite the modest title is the equivalent of a star pastry chef. (The profession was once exclusively female.) An accomplished *smørrebrød* maker knows how to prepare all of the components for each sandwich and assemble them correctly. Some of the most famous patterns include Shooting Star (fried plaice with prawns and asparagus spears, often topped with caviar), Veterinarians' Midnight Snack (liver pâté, beef aspic, boiled salted veal, and onion), H. C. Andersen (crisp bacon topped with liver pâté and tomato and garnished with freshly grated horseradish and aspic) and my own favorite, Sun over Gudhjem (smoked herring and chives with a glistening raw egg yolk on top).

Even the most modern, architectural iterations of *smørrebrød* stem from the peasant fare that workers took out into the fields for lunch—slices of dense, whole-grain rye bread (*brød*) spread with a generous smear of salted butter (*smør*) and covered with a *pålæg*, or topping. These sandwiches were so convenient that the word *rugbrødsmad* (literally, "rye bread meal") is sometimes used as a kind of shorthand for "lunch." The sturdy rye platform for the *smørrebrød* likely evolved from the medieval trenchers of bread. But what started out as a simple, functional meal turned fashionable in the late nineteenth century, thanks to the wife of a Copenhagen wine merchant who allegedly convinced her husband that he needed to serve food at his wine tastings. In 1888 the wine merchant Oskar Davidsen opened his eponymous restaurant, which by the early twentieth century was offering 178 different sandwiches on an attention-grabbing menu four-and-a-half feet long. *Smørrebrød* were also offered at the city's elegant Tivoli Gardens, and soon country food became elegant fare. Unlike

their country cousins, *smørrebrød* in the city were—and still are—eaten with knife and fork.

As with the Swedish *smörgåsbord*, *smørrebrød* should be consumed in several courses, in a prescribed order. Herring comes first, then other fish, followed by meat and finally cheese. Plenty of aquavit washes down each course. Restaurants typically display prototypes of each sandwich so that customers can choose whatever appeals most. (Sadly, the beautiful spreads of old are less visually thrilling today, now that EU regulations require the food to be covered with plastic wrap.) A newfangled type of *smørrebrød* is *smushi*, which unlike the traditional large sandwiches are meant to be eaten in small bites, like sushi. And while Danish households don't come equipped with their own sandwich maids, people sometimes throw a *smørrebrød* party by setting out bowls of different components for guests to construct their own sandwiches.

For Americans, the food most synonymous with Denmark is Danish pastry, even though the Danish name for these divine baked goods, *wienerbrød*, reflects their Viennese origins.

The exact circumstances of their arrival in Denmark remain a little murky. We know that in the mid-nineteenth century Danish bakers went abroad to perfect their baking skills and discovered yeasted, butter-rich dough in Vienna. Or perhaps the defining moment came more suddenly, in 1850, when Austrian bakers were imported to Copenhagen to fill in for the Danish bakers who had gone on strike. In any case, the Danes made their own adaptations to Viennese pastry by adding more egg to the modified puff paste and filling the dough with their beloved *remonce*, a mixture of butter and sugar and sometimes marzipan. In the early twentieth century these "Danish" pastries landed in the United States. Lauritz C. Klitteng, a baker from Læsø, claims to have baked Danish pastries for the 1915 wedding of President Woodrow Wilson and Edith Galt. Though that menu remains undocumented, we know for sure that within five years Klitteng had capitalized on the pastry's chicness by founding the Danish Culinary Studio on New York's Fifth Avenue. Danish pastries were apparently as much a sensation then as New Nordic cooking is today.

A 1917 article in the *Oakland Tribune* enthused, "With the Danish pastry—you just tuck a small morsel under the tongue, roll up the eyes, say 'Ah-h' as though there were a sky-rocket present, and it fades away and trickles down to the barbed-wire entanglements of the soul, a subtle something that clings like an opium eater's dream."

I get more kick from eating *æbleskiver*, small pancake puffs that, unlike Danish pastry, are Danish through and through. The leavened batter is poured into a special cast-iron pan with seven round indentations. After one side cooks, the pancakes are carefully turned with a skewer or fork tine to form adorable spheres. Southern Denmark is famous for its apples, and these pancakes originally contained diced apples or a spoonful of applesauce. I hope someday to try *svupsak*, a regional variation from the southern islands of Lolland and Falster that calls for opening the pancakes and pouring in some schnapps before popping them into your mouth.

Another old-fashioned dessert is gingerbread, which the Danes adore, especially in winter, when its warming spices echo those used in the season's mulled wine. Thanks to active maritime trade beginning with the Vikings, exotic spices were available to those who could afford them, and ginger, cinnamon, cardamom, and cloves enhanced many older Danish dishes. A particular breakfast specialty was *øllebrød med fløde*, based on the principle of the hair of the dog: beer is simmered with toasted rye bread crumbs, spices, and cream into a nourishing dish for the morning after.

The use of spices increased in early modern times, when the vast reaches of the Danish East India Company, and later the Asiatic Company, made them more affordable. Chartered in 1616, the Danish East India Company traded silver for spices, establishing its first outpost in Tranquebar, on India's east coast (Tranquebar remained a Danish colony until 1845). In 1732 the Asiatic Company began trading with Canton, China, to import porcelain and tea in addition to spices. Beginning in the mid-seventeenth century, Denmark was also active in the New World, colonizing St. Thomas, St. John, and St. Croix in the Caribbean, which became known as the Danish West Indies (they're now the U.S. Virgin Islands). There, like other colonial powers, Denmark oversaw brutal sugar plantations that relied on slave labor to harvest and process the cane sent to Copenhagen for refining. Along with the sugar, the West Indies trade brought vanilla and allspice to the Danish kitchen, where both flavorings became mainstays.

The sea has been important to Danish cuisine in other, more local ways. As an island nation, Denmark has 4,500 miles of coastline on the North Sea and the Baltic that provides easy access to fish and shellfish. The Danes especially love the blue mussels that grow in the tidal flats of the Wadden Sea and the meaty Limfjord oysters. Herring has long been enjoyed, fried fresh in season or pickled, in which guise it often appears on *smørrebrød*. Tiny, sweet fjord shrimp are likewise perfect as sandwich toppings. Fish cakes are a popular supper dish, served with lightly curried remoulade, a now-classic Danish sauce that reflects Denmark's colonial rule in India. Oily mackerel is balanced with a tart rhubarb sauce, while mild flatfish like plaice are lightly fried and served with boiled potatoes and parsley sauce. The combination of fried fish, boiled potatoes, and parsley sauce is found all along the Danish coast at the traditional inns known as *kroer*. Because Danish dairies produced abundant butter and milk, it made sense to put them together in a rich, béchamel-like sauce (one of the few direct borrowings from classical French cuisine) to serve with the catch of the day. White sauce is also spooned over boiled peas and carrots, although current taste more often enables the vegetables to shine on their own.

One distinctive coastal fish dish is *bakskuld*, dab or plaice that has been salted, dried, and then cold-smoked. Like Norway's dried cod, *bakskuld* keeps for a very long time, but unlike the cod it isn't soaked before eating. To serve, the head and tail of the fish are removed and the tough skin is pulled off to expose the flesh. The fish is then divided into four fillets, which are placed in a pan with plenty of salted butter to sauté until just warm. Each fillet is set on a piece of well-buttered rye bread and washed down with a goodly amount of beer and aquavit—a potent triad of sea, salt, and grain. Modern diners often add a dollop of remoulade sauce and some squeezes of lemon.

Given the traditional conservatism of Danish food, it's exhilarating to find Denmark at the vanguard of the New Nordic movement. Stockholm and Helsinki once outdid Copenhagen with their grand enclosed markets dating back more than a hundred years. But no more. Now Copenhagen has the Torvehallerne, a pair of magnificent food halls that opened in 2011, with stalls featuring the extraordinary produce of Bornholm, apple wine and cherry spirits from Denmark's temperate south, and an array of local beers. The country's food culture is evolving in exciting ways, rapidly, and no longer in glacial time. Farms like Aarstiderne and Fuglebjerggaard are spreading the gospel of organic produce to wean Danes from so much pork and dairy. Aarstiderne's founder Søren Ejlersen is working to change the diet through taste and the senses, what he calls "a dance between the planet and the people." At Fuglebjerggaard, Camilla Plum is planting heirloom vegetables and fruits and creating a Nordic seed bank that focuses on foods that thrive in the region and that can be harvested in the field, not just foraged. Many schools incorporate gardens into their curricula, and there are even "nature preschools," where understanding natural processes like raising and slaughtering chickens is considered essential to child development. And in typically Danish fashion, everything is being done with style, from clever *smørrebrød* lunchboxes with four compartments (Danish bento boxes!) to farm-grown vegetable shares distributed not in paper sacks or cardboard but in wooden boxes that are simply but beautifully crafted. Even as the modern imperatives of health and radical tastes move to the fore, the Danish culinary aesthetic remains true to simplicity and practicality as it redefines tradition and expands the range of flavors that the Danes can enjoy.

FISH + SHELLFISH

Four icy seas surround Scandinavia: the Baltic, the North, the Norwegian, and the Barents. When you add in the region's many rivers and freshwater lakes, it's easy to see why fish and seafood are mainstays of the northern diet. Fish like herring, salmon, mackerel, lake trout, and whitefish provide copious amounts of omega-3 fatty acids, in addition to protein and vitamins, so they were historically crucial for maintaining health in a climate where few vegetables thrived. Mussels, oysters, shrimp, and other shellfish similarly deliver plentiful nutrients. But the reason contemporary Scandinavians eat so much fish and seafood has more to do with deliciousness. In summer they may toss the day's catch into a pot over a fire on the beach, or grill it on a roasting stick, or prepare fire-glow salmon by nailing the fillet to a plank and letting it roast in the fire's radiant heat. In wintertime, when cooking moves indoors, small stovetop smokers stoked with alder chips are used.

The Nordic kitchen is justifiably famous for its preserved fish. Gravlax (cured salmon) and pickled herring are widely familiar, but why not try ice-cellar salmon, a Finnish method of brining that keeps the flesh delicate and moist? Or you can give a basic shrimp boil a Nordic twist by adding plenty of dill, or treat cod or mussels to freshly grated horseradish. Other common Scandinavian fish also deserve more attention in the States. Pike may have bones to contend with, but it's dazzling when oven-roasted with wild mushrooms. Ocean perch is divine when lightly smoked and served with herbed sour cream. Most neglected of all is fresh herring, which Americans once relished. Sadly, the bulk of the U.S. herring catch is now exported or turned into pet food (at least cats still consider herring a delicacy). It's worth making friends with a fishmonger to get fresh herring in season. Marinate the fillets lightly and spread them with a mustardy mayonnaise, or drizzle them with a lively sweet-and-sour sauce. Sometimes simplest is best: dredged with fine rye meal and turned in a pan of sizzling butter, lightly fried herring is a delight.

GRAVLAX IS ONE of the glories of Nordic cuisine, found throughout Scandinavia. The name is an abbreviated form of *gravad lax*, or buried salmon. As a means of preservation, the fish used to be cured underground, where it fermented slightly. Each Nordic country has its own style of curing the salmon, I have opted for the proportions most commonly used in Sweden, where sugar is king: two parts sugar to one part salt. Just make sure to use a coarse sea salt and not fine table salt, or the fish will turn out too salty.

When I first started making gravlax, long ago, I was afraid that the salmon wouldn't properly "cook," so I assiduously followed the typical directions for curing it for 48 hours or more, sandwiching dill between salmon fillets and pressing them under a weight to draw out the moisture. But I have since come to appreciate a much fresher tasting salmon that is cured just long enough to gain a buttery texture without losing the intrinsic flavor of the fish. After the gravlax is ready, you can rinse off the curing mixture, and keep the fish in the refrigerator for several more days or freeze it for a few weeks.

I like to vary my gravlax according to season. In the early spring, when the first buds appear on the birch and spruce trees, I pick a handful to mix in with the dill. And in the summer, fresh elderflowers add a lovely floral note.

Gravlax

 # SALT- AND SUGAR-CURED SALMON

SERVES 10

1 large bunch dill, plus 2 cups coarsely chopped dill stems and leaves

1 (3-pound) best-quality salmon side, scaled, with skin on

1 cup sugar

½ cup coarse sea salt

2 tablespoons cracked white peppercorns

1 tablespoon coriander seeds, crushed

Mustard Sauce (see recipe, page 132)

Set a shallow glass or enamel baking pan large enough to hold the salmon on the counter. Line the bottom of the pan with the sprigs from 1 bunch of dill. Place the salmon fillet on top of the dill, skin side down.

In a bowl, stir together the sugar, salt, peppercorns, and coriander seeds, and rub gently into the salmon flesh. Sprinkle the chopped dill over the sugar mixture. Cover with plastic wrap and let sit at cool room temperature for 8 hours, then refrigerate for 24 hours. Quickly rinse off the curing mixture and pat the fish dry. Serve cold, very thinly sliced, with mustard sauce.

NOTE: Americans tend to lay smoked or cured salmon out in flat slices, but the Nordic presentation is more dramatic: Roll each thin slice of gravlax into a swirl, like a rosebud, and place it upright on the serving platter.

CONTINUED

MUSTARD SAUCE

3 tablespoons Swedish-style mustard

2 tablespoons white wine vinegar (or less, to taste)

½ cup canola oil

½ cup finely chopped fresh dill

2 to 3 teaspoons sugar

Salt

Mustard sauce is the classic complement to gravlax. The Swedes have been mixing mustard, vinegar, and oil together for centuries, but these days the dressing is sweetened with sugar and enlivened with dill. Some like their sauce on the sweet side, others prefer it more sour. The recipe below yields a sauce with a nice vinegary tang and just a hint of sweetness. It's worth seeking out mild Swedish-style mustard (see Sources), but a mixture of honey and Dijon mustards can always be substituted to get the right balance. Just keep tasting and adjusting until the sauce suits your palate.

Stir together the mustard and vinegar in a small bowl, then whisk in the oil until an emulsion forms. Stir in the dill, 2 teaspoons of the sugar, and a pinch of salt. Taste and season with more sugar and salt as needed. Refrigerate for at least a couple of hours before serving to allow the flavors to meld.

THIS SIMPLE BUT exciting dish was another gift from Tommy Henriksson at Melander's Fisk in Stockholm. It has remained one of our favorite ways to prepare cod. The summer after our year in Stockholm, we hopscotched on mail boats along the north coast of Norway, where cod was drying on great racks as far as the eye could see. Norway was (and to some degree still is) defined by its superlative and abundant cod, even though there, as elsewhere, the fish has become more of a luxury due to habitat loss and overfishing.

In Sweden we made this dish with cod steaks, but we've had to adapt the recipe to fillets, since steaks are just about impossible to find. Our fishmonger explained that they've largely disappeared from the market because cutting steaks entails too much waste. And certainly cod is too precious to waste.

The rule of thumb for cooking fish is 10 minutes per inch. If you have a fillet that's ¾ inch thick—a perfect size for this recipe—it will take 7 to 8 minutes in the pan. Just be sure not to overcook the fish—it should remain succulent and moist. The proportions below are based on a 1-pound fillet, so if you're cooking more, adjust the ingredients and timing accordingly. We like to serve this cod with parsleyed beets from the garden and boiled new potatoes tossed with a little butter and dill.

Torsk med pepperrot

 # NORWEGIAN-STYLE COD
WITH HORSERADISH

SERVES 2 TO 4

2 tablespoons butter
2 teaspoons vegetable oil
1 pound cod fillet
1 teaspoon salt
½ cup freshly grated horseradish

Heat the butter and oil in a large cast-iron skillet over medium-high heat until the butter begins to brown. Throw down ½ teaspoon of salt into the hot pan and immediately place the fish over it. Sprinkle the top of the fish with the remaining ½ teaspoon of salt. Cover the skillet (if your skillet does not have a lid, use a lid from another pot or aluminum foil) and cook over medium-high heat until the fish begins to look opaque, about 4 minutes.

Remove the lid, and with a spatula as long as the fillet, carefully flip the fish. Sprinkle the horseradish over the fish and lower the heat to medium. To be sure the fish doesn't burn, it's a good idea to check that there is enough fat remaining in the pan; add a bit more butter if necessary. Re-cover the pan and continue to cook 3 to 4 minutes more, until the fish is flaky but still moist. Using the large spatula, carefully transfer the fish to a platter. Serve immediately.

WHEN I MAKE Finnish salmon soup I remove the skin and turn it into a savory snack or a garnish for open-faced sandwiches. Fried in just a hint of oil, it turns out beautifully crisp. Don't worry if some of the salmon flesh clings to the skin when you remove it—that makes for a more colorful presentation.

Rapeaksi paistettu lohennahka

CRISP-FRIED SALMON SKIN

SERVES 4

Skin from a 1-pound salmon fillet
Salt
Vegetable oil, for frying

With a sharp fillet knife, carefully remove the skin from the salmon in a single piece and pat dry with a paper towel. Sprinkle it on both sides with a little salt.

Pour a thin coating of vegetable oil into a large cast-iron skillet and heat over medium-high heat. Place the salmon skin in the skillet flesh side up, and lower the heat to medium. Use a spatula to press the skin down to keep it from curling. Fry the skin until it is crisp on the bottom, 4 to 5 minutes, periodically sliding a spatula underneath it to make sure it doesn't stick. Then flip the skin and fry skin up for 4 to 5 minutes more. Flip it again so the skin is face down, then roll it up with the fleshy part inside. Transfer the roll to a serving plate and cut it into ½-inch slices. Serve hot or at room temperature.

FISH CAKES APPEAR in various guises throughout the Nordic lands. Originally considered poor man's food, they are an excellent way to use scraps of fish that might otherwise go to waste. The surprise in this Danish version is its gorgeous green hue, a gift from the fresh herbs that are mixed in. When the fish cakes are topped with yellow remoulade, the dish is wonderfully colorful on the plate.

Danish remoulade offers a good example of the culinary adoption process. Through its shipping empire, Denmark had access to exotic spices. Danes took a particular liking to curry powder, which they often combine with a classic remoulade sauce, itself adopted from French cuisine. The addition of yellow mustard and curry powder to the mayonnaise turns the sauce a vivid yellow.

Fiskefrikadeller med remoulade

FISH CAKES
WITH REMOULADE SAUCE
SERVES 4

1 small yellow onion, coarsely chopped

1 pound cod or other whitefish, skin removed and cut into 1-inch pieces

½ cup chopped fresh dill

½ cup chopped fresh parsley

¼ cup flour

1 egg, lightly beaten

2 tablespoons melted butter, plus 1 tablespoon

1 teaspoon salt

½ teaspoon freshly ground pepper

2 tablespoons vegetable oil

Remoulade Sauce (see recipe, page 138)

Process the onion finely in the bowl of a food processor. Add the fish, dill, parsley, flour, egg, 2 tablespoons of melted butter, salt, and pepper and pulse until ground medium fine. Transfer the mixture to a bowl and refrigerate, covered, for at least 1 hour and up to 4 hours (the longer you refrigerate the fish mixture, the greener the fish cakes will be).

Shape the fish mixture into 8 patties. Set them on waxed paper.

Heat the oil and the remaining 1 tablespoon of butter in a heavy, wide skillet over medium heat. When the butter begins to foam, add the fish cakes and cook for about 6 minutes, until golden, periodically sliding a spatula under the cakes to make sure they don't stick. Carefully flip the fish cakes, lower the heat to medium-low, and continue cooking until nicely browned, about 6 minutes more, periodically using the spatula to keep the fish cakes from sticking. Serve immediately, with remoulade sauce on the side.

CONTINUED

FISH CAKES WITH REMOULADE SAUCE

CONTINUED

REMOULADE SAUCE

½ cup mayonnaise

¼ cup minced dill pickle

1 tablespoon capers, rinsed and drained

1 tablespoon snipped fresh chives

½ teaspoon minced fresh tarragon

½ teaspoon prepared yellow mustard

¼ teaspoon curry powder

⅛ teaspoon salt

Freshly ground white pepper

Make this sauce ahead of time and refrigerate for a few hours to give the flavors a chance to blend and the mayonnaise time to absorb the color of the curry powder and mustard.

Stir together all of the ingredients in a small bowl. Scrape into a serving dish and refrigerate until well chilled.

THIS RECIPE COMES directly from the cellar of Maria Planting. Although I've been a gravlax fan since, well, forever, I actually like this method of brining salmon better than gravlax. I feel like a heretic! The fish can be eaten after a mere twenty-four hours, when it will be elegant and silken, but Maria generally brines it for three or four days. I've decided I like it best at two days, after the flavor has deepened but hasn't lost its fresh taste. If you're making the salmon in the spring, you can toss a handful of spruce tips into the brine for additional flavor.

Jääkellarilohi

ICE CELLAR SALMON

SERVES 4

4 cups water

½ cup coarse sea salt

¼ cup sugar

1 tablespoon caraway seeds

1 tablespoon allspice berries

1 large bunch dill, very coarsely chopped

1½ pounds center-cut salmon fillet

Mustard Sauce (page 132)

In a large pot, combine the water, salt, sugar, caraway, and allspice. Bring to a boil and let boil for a few minutes, until the salt and sugar dissolve. Remove from the heat and stir in the chopped dill. Set aside to cool to room temperature.

Place the salmon, flesh side down, in the room-temperature brine (if necessary, place a weight on top of the salmon to keep it immersed). Refrigerate, covered, for 2 days. Remove the fish from the brine, rinse quickly under cold water, and pat dry. Slice thin, and serve cold with mustard sauce.

UNTIL WE MOVED to Stockholm, I had never tasted fresh herring, a fish once so abundant along the East Coast that a Boston parkway and T stop are named after the local river variety. That's not, of course, the Herring Parkway, but the Alewife—a name that also reminds us how well this fish goes with beer! The Atlantic herring once swam in vast numbers all up and down the East Coast, as the Pacific herring did in the West. But like so much other seafood, it fell victim to overfishing. Today's fisheries are highly regulated. Most of the catch goes for tuna and lobster bait, or it's exported to countries that appreciate the fresh fish. And that's a shame, because herring is one of the most delicious fish I know.

Fresh herring is enjoyed widely throughout Scandinavia, but in the States we must wait for the annual herring run (late spring in the Northeast; winter in the San Francisco Bay Area). And each year I make frantic phone calls to ensure that I get my share, often ordering ten pounds at a time. Most goes for pickling but I always set aside enough to prepare a few special fresh herring dishes, like this one. This Swedish preparation translates as "herring flounder," because the small fish are butterflied to resemble flat flounder fillets. Be warned, though: once you try fresh herring, you'll be hooked, finding yourself eagerly watching the calendar till the next herring season rolls around.

Strömmingsflundror

FRESH HERRING
IN THE STYLE OF FLOUNDER
SERVES 2 TO 4

1 pound fresh herring (about 4)

3 tablespoons butter, at room temperature, plus 1 tablespoon

½ cup chopped fresh herbs (such as parsley, dill, chives, chervil, and tarragon)

Scant 1 teaspoon salt

2 tablespoons rye meal or coarse rye flour

2 tablespoons vegetable oil

With a sharp knife, remove the heads and tails of the fish. Slit the belly and remove the innards, then carefully peel off the backbone, leaving a hinged fillet. All of the bones should come with it; if a few tiny bones remain, it's not a problem, as they virtually melt with the cooking. Rinse the fish and pat dry with paper towels. Set aside on a plate, skin side down.

In a small bowl, cream the 3 tablespoons of room-temperature butter with the chopped herbs. Sprinkle the fillets with salt, then spread the herb butter on the flesh side of two of them. With the flesh sides facing each other, cover each fillet with one of the remaining pieces of herring to make a kind of sandwich.

Spread the rye meal or flour in a shallow dish and dredge the fillet "sandwiches" on both sides until well coated. Shake off the excess. Heat the oil and the remaining 1 tablespoon of butter in a large skillet over medium-high heat. When sizzling, add the herring and sauté, flipping once, until golden on both sides, about 6 minutes total. Serve hot.

VARIATION: I love the depth of flavor that rye meal adds, but if you prefer a richer, more delicate taste you can batter the herring. Dip the fillets in 1 lightly beaten egg, and then in 2 tablespoons of fine dried bread crumbs to coat. Sauté as directed above.

CRAYFISH

If the Fourth of July is our big summer celebration, in Sweden and Finland it's the opening of crayfish season. Beginning in late July and into August, family and friends mark this yearly ritual with *kräftskivor*, crayfish parties, consuming the beloved crustaceans by the dozens, washing them down with plenty of beer and schnapps and singing celebratory songs.

The Scandinavian love of this particular shellfish is, in some ways, surprising, as its introduction to the table was anything but auspicious. The sixteenth-century scientist Peder Månsson advocated crayfish as a cholera preventative, recommending a tincture of crayfish dissolved in distilled alcohol. For his part, the great taxonomist Carl Linnaeus warned against eating shellfish of any kind (it turns out he was allergic). But crayfish proved a good source of income for country folk, who trapped and sold them for the enjoyment of the wealthy. Crayfish eventually became so well loved that the satirist Albert Engström used them to oppose a pending Prohibition law in 1922. He designed a poster declaring "NO! Crayfish require these drinks! You must abstain from crayfish if you don't vote no on August 27th." The association between indulging in crayfish and imbibing continues to this day.

Crayfish were so popular that by the early twentieth century their numbers had dwindled alarmingly, so governments imposed restrictions, limiting the catch to only a few months each year. Things got worse in 1907, when a fungus infected the native noble crayfish (*Astacus astacus*), causing a still-devastating crayfish plague. The remedy proved worse than the disease. In the 1960s, American signal crayfish (*Pacifastacus leniusculus*) were introduced, and not only did they turn out to be carriers of the fungus, they also began to crowd out the native species. So great is the demand for crayfish–Sweden is Europe's largest importer–that crayfish are now imported from the United States and China, but the indigenous, local species is still preferred. Each summer those with enough money gladly pay for the privilege to eat the native noble crayfish, which they deem superior in taste.

BECAUSE CRAYFISH PARTIES are such an institution, no Nordic cookbook would be complete without a crayfish recipe. On the other hand, I can't enjoy the frozen ones that most of us in the States have to settle for. So I've decided to riff on the traditional recipe and adapt it to shrimp instead. I use an oatmeal stout for especially rich flavor. Look for flowering dill at farmer's markets, where it's often displayed next to pickling cucumbers. When serving the shrimp, be sure to offer plenty of crispbread and cheese (not to mention beer and schnapps) on the side.

Räkor med krondill

>>> SHRIMP <<<
IN THE STYLE OF CRAYFISH

SERVES 4

3 pounds jumbo unpeeled shrimp (10/15 count)

6 cups cold water

3 cups stout (or one 22-ounce bottle)

4 tablespoons salt

2 tablespoons sugar

2 tablespoons dill seed

8 large flowering crowns of dill

With kitchen shears, snip the backs of the shrimp from head to tail, then rinse out the veins under cold water.

Bring the cold water, beer, salt, sugar, and dill seed to a boil in a large stockpot. Drop the shrimp into the boiling brine and immediately turn off the heat. Toss in the flowering crowns of dill, stirring to submerge them, then cover the pot. Let the shrimp sit in the brine at room temperature for 6 to 8 hours. To serve, remove the shrimp from the brine and mound on a large platter.

THE HORSERADISH PLANT in our garden is out of control—it's easily two feet tall and three feet wide—but I love this fiery root that spreads mysteriously underground. The Scandinavians use horseradish creatively, in all sorts of ways. Here, in a Nordic riff on the classic French *moules marinières*, mussels are steamed in caraway-scented aquavit and finished off with a zesty dose of fresh horseradish.

Muslinger med peberrod

MUSSELS
WITH HORSERADISH CREAM

SERVES 2 TO 4

2 tablespoons butter

1 large shallot, minced

1¼ cups aquavit

2 pounds mussels, cleaned

3 tablespoons heavy cream

2 to 3 tablespoons freshly grated horseradish, depending on the pungency, plus shaved horseradish for garnish

2 tablespoons minced fresh parsley

Freshly ground white pepper

Melt the butter in a large stockpot over medium-low heat, add the shallot, and sauté until soft but not brown, 2 to 3 minutes. Pour in the aquavit, then add the mussels. Cover the pot, bring to a boil over medium-high heat, and cook until the mussels open wide, 5 to 7 minutes, depending on their size. Turn off the heat and discard any mussels that didn't open. With a slotted spoon, transfer the mussels to a large serving bowl.

Bring the cooking liquid in the pot to a boil over medium-high heat and cook until slightly reduced, about 2 minutes. Lower the heat, add the cream, horseradish, and parsley, and simmer until the flavors blend, about 2 minutes. Generously grind white pepper over the top just before you pour off the sauce.

Pour the sauce over the mussels in the serving bowl. Serve garnished with shaved horseradish.

THIS RECIPE COMES from Helge Semb, a retired video photographer who looks like a Viking and cooks like a dream. Helge spends summers at a beautiful off-the-grid cabin he and his wife, Berit, built on an isolated fjord in Brønnøysund, Norway. Getting to the cabin requires a small trek, a mile's walk through mossy terrain that's abundant with wild blueberries in July and lingonberries in late August. Our dinners there captured the flavors of the Norwegian coast—local salmon smoked over juniper branches; grilled Arctic mountain lamb, aromatic with wild herbs. We lingered outside long after our meals ended, reluctant to turn our backs on the midnight sun and the vivid colors of the sky. One night Helge decided to stroll over to a small pond where he'd spotted a trout the previous day. There it was again! With a masterful swoop of the net he caught the trout, and we had fresh fish for breakfast the next morning.

Helge's batter provides a wonderfully light, crisp coating, thanks to the baking powder and the carbonation of the beer. This recipe is excellent with any mild lake fish—just make sure it is achingly fresh.

Fritert fisk

 CRISP FRIED FISH

SERVES 4

1 (12-ounce) bottle dark or amber ale

1½ cups flour

2 tablespoons cornstarch

2 teaspoons baking powder

2 pounds trout or whitefish fillets

Vegetable oil, for frying

Salt and freshly ground pepper

To make the batter, stir together the beer, flour, cornstarch, and baking powder in a wide bowl. Let sit for 30 to 45 minutes.

To fry the fish, cut each fillet in half and pat dry with paper towels. In a large skillet, pour the oil to a depth of ¼ inch. The oil is hot enough when a droplet of water tossed onto it sizzles.

Sprinkle the fish liberally with salt and pepper on both sides, then dip into the batter, making sure that the fish is completely coated. Gently place the fish skin side down in the hot oil, sliding a spatula under each piece after 30 seconds to make sure the fish doesn't stick. Fry until golden, about 3 minutes, then carefully flip and fry until golden on the other side, about 2 minutes more. Remove from the oil with the spatula or tongs and serve immediately.

I FEEL VERY fortunate to have met Jarmo Pitkänen, who opened Studio Restaurant Tundra in the mountains of Finnish Lapland ten years ago. The isolated town of Kuusamo may seem like an unusual place to site a fine restaurant, but after many years of cooking abroad, Jarmo wanted to return to the North, where he grew up, to raise his five daughters in the mountains' wild beauty. He constructed a two-story building with a small but ideal restaurant kitchen and elegant private-dining space on the top floor. His pottery studio, where he fashions the restaurant's stylish tableware, is located below. Jarmo cooks in the New Nordic style, making use of the North's surprising abundance and tweaking traditional recipes to suit modern taste.

When my husband and I visited, Jarmo invited us into the kitchen to help prepare our meal, sharing his deep knowledge of the region's flavors. And what a feast we had! We began with a salad of reindeer tongue seasoned with vinegar, grated horseradish, garlic, and local canola oil. Next came a Finnish classic, salmon soup, followed by fresh pike fillets lightly coated with rye meal and fried quickly in butter. We put the remaining pike through a meat grinder and served it over boiled potatoes, with fresh peas, trout roe, and tiny greens from his garden. We then seared a fillet of black grouse that Jarmo had hunted himself; he served it rare with a sauce of wild mushrooms and shallots. We finished up with perch, freshly caught from the nearby lake, which we smoked briefly on the stovetop over alder chips, adding a few drops of *tervakusi* ("tar pee," Jarmo's playful name for tar extract) to enhance the smoky flavor.

Jarmo swears by his stovetop smoker (see Sources), since it allows him to enjoy a taste of the outdoors even in the depths of winter, and now we're hooked by this cooking method too. It's a carefree way to achieve moist, flavorful fish—even without tar pee.

Savustettua lohta

 SMOKED ARCTIC CHAR

SERVES 2 OR 3, OR MORE AS AN APPETIZER

1 teaspoon peppercorns, cracked

2 tablespoons juniper berries, crushed

3 cups water

2 tablespoons salt

2 tablespoons sugar

1 arctic char fillet with skin on, about 1 pound

To make a brine, add peppercorns, juniper berries, water, salt, and sugar to a large saucepan. Bring to a boil and cook just until the sugar and salt dissolve. Pour the hot brine into a shallow dish that's large enough to hold the fish and set aside to cool to room temperature.

Place the fish, flesh side down, in the cooled brine. Let sit at room temperature for 1 hour.

CONTINUED

SMOKED ARCTIC CHAR
CONTINUED

Prepare a stovetop smoker according to the manufacturer's directions—they're easy and precise about how to mound the wood chips and regulate the heat on different types of burners. With a paper towel, wipe the spices from the fish and place it on the smoker rack, skin side down. Smoke the fish over alder chips for 25 minutes. Serve hot or refrigerate up to 2 days for later use.

VARIATION: An old-fashioned practice from the Swedish country-side called *dopp i kopp*—"dip in the cup"—is not so different from our custom of serving lobster with a butter dipping sauce. For each serving of *dopp i kopp*, simply melt some butter over low heat and pour it into a coffee cup, preferably a charming old one with a crackled glaze. Stir in minced fresh chives and dill, and a pinch of salt, and set the cup on a plate with some of the smoked char. Complete the meal with boiled new potatoes, also excellent for dipping.

THE MINGLING OF sweet and sour is a bedrock principle of the Nordic kitchen, especially in southern Sweden and Denmark, where this dish is very popular. Many recipes recommend leaving the herring in the marinade for several days, but I find that the vinegar tends to overwhelm the fish, so I prefer it freshly made. If you do decide to marinate the fish for a few days, be sure to bring it to room temperature before serving, and add the herbs just before serving, too, so that they don't wilt. The herbal garnish–suggested by Denmark's food maven Camilla Plum–makes for a gorgeous presentation. Any leftovers are excellent on crispbread.

Ättiksströmming

SWEET-AND-SOUR HERRING

SERVES 2 TO 4

¼ cup cider vinegar

2½ tablespoons sugar

1½ teaspoons salt

¼ teaspoon freshly ground pepper

1 pound fresh herring (about 4)

2 tablespoons coarse-ground mustard

2 tablespoons coarse rye flour

3 tablespoons butter

1 small red onion, thinly sliced

1 tablespoon freshly grated horseradish

½ cup chopped fresh herbs (such as parsley, dill, chives, tarragon, and chervil)

To make the sweet-and-sour sauce, bring the vinegar, sugar, ¼ teaspoon of the salt, and the pepper to a boil in a small saucepan, stirring to dissolve the salt and sugar. Set aside to cool to lukewarm.

With a sharp knife, remove the heads and tails of the fish. Slit the belly and remove the innards, then carefully peel off the backbone, leaving a hinged fillet. Rinse the fish and pat dry with paper towels. Set aside on a plate, skin side down.

Sprinkle each fillet with ¼ teaspoon of the salt and spread each one with 1½ teaspoons of the mustard. Fold each fillet in half to enclose the mustard and set aside.

Mix the rye flour with the remaining ¼ teaspoon of salt. Spread the flour mixture in a shallow dish and dredge the fillets on both sides until well coated. Shake off the excess. Melt the butter in a large skillet over medium-high heat. When the butter sizzles, add the fillets and sauté for approximately 3 minutes on each side, until golden.

Transfer the fillets to a serving plate that can accommodate liquid. Let cool for 5 minutes, then pour the sweet-and-sour sauce over the fish. Top with the onion and horseradish, and generously strew the herbs over all. Eat warm or at room temperature, making sure to spoon a little extra sauce over the top of each serving.

THE DELICIOUSNESS OF this dish depends on the quality of the ingredients you use. Like so many Nordic preparations, the recipe is as basic as nature itself. You combine river (pike), forest (mushrooms), and earth (herbs). If, like me, you don't live near any cold bodies of water, you'll need to ask your fishmonger to order a whole, gutted pike. For the mushrooms, chanterelles, hen-of-the-woods, and black trumpets are especially flavorful, but in a pinch you can use shiitake, oyster mushrooms, and portobellos. If all the components are fresh, this dish will dazzle. Baked pike often graces the Christmas table in the Finnish archipelago.

Uunihaukea sienten ja pinaatin kera

BAKED PIKE
WITH MUSHROOMS AND SPINACH

SERVES 4

1 yellow onion, finely chopped

3 cloves garlic, finely chopped

2 tablespoons unsalted butter

12 ounces wild mushrooms, trimmed and finely chopped

1 cup cooked spinach, squeezed dry and chopped

¼ cup minced fresh herbs (such as parsley, dill, chives, and chervil)

½ teaspoon salt, plus more for rubbing

Freshly ground pepper

1 whole pike, about 2 to 2½ pounds, scaled and gutted

2 or 3 thick slices bacon

In a large skillet over medium-low heat, sauté the onion and garlic in 1 tablespoon of the butter until golden, 6 to 8 minutes. Add the remaining tablespoon of butter to the pan, then stir in the mushrooms. Continue to cook over medium-low heat for 10 minutes, stirring occasionally, until the mushrooms are cooked through and all of the moisture evaporates. Stir in the spinach, herbs, and salt. Season with pepper and stir again until well combined.

Preheat the oven to 425°F. Rinse the fish and pat dry with paper towels. Rub the fish liberally with salt and pepper all over, inside and out, then fill the cavity with the mushroom mixture (reserve the leftover mushroom mixture for garnish). Either sew the cavity shut with kitchen twine or use trussing skewers.

Butter a large roasting pan and place the fish in it. Lay 2 or 3 strips of bacon lengthwise over the fish to moisten it as it bakes.

Roast for 25 to 30 minutes, until the fish is flaky. Remove the twine or skewers. Transfer the fish to a platter and spoon any leftover mushroom mixture decoratively around it. To carve the fish, use a fish knife and fork to remove the skin, then slide the knife along the backbone to free the top fillet. Cut the fillet in half and transfer the pieces to serving plates, along with some mushroom filling. Then lift off the backbone to reveal the second fillet. Cut it in half and plate.

IDEALLY YOU SHOULD experience this succulent, slow-roasted salmon the way we first did, in Finnish Lapland, in a yurt, with the fire glowing in the half-light. But on the off chance that you don't have a yurt or a fire pit in your backyard, I've adapted this traditional Sami method for a charcoal kettle grill.

The only additional equipment you'll need is a cedar plank and nongalvanized, noncoated nails. The plank infuses the fish with a subtly smoky flavor; it can be cleaned and reused a number of times. As for the cooking, it's best scheduled for a leisurely occasion, since it requires several steps and culminates in an hour's attention to the fire. You may want to do as I do, and assign the cooking to the Prometheus in your household.

Loimulohi

 # FIRE-GLOW SALMON

SERVES 6

1 (3-pound) salmon fillet

4 cups water

3 tablespoons salt

You'll also need about 2 quarts of all-natural charcoal briquettes and eight 1- to 2-inch chunks of bark-free grilling wood, such as alder, apple, cedar, or oak

About 3 hours before serving time, soak a cedar plank long enough to accommodate the salmon in water (we soak it in a heavy trash bag laid out on the lawn). The cedar plank should be about 6 inches longer than the fillet.

Next, make a brine. Bring the water and salt to a boil in a large pot. Pour the hot brine into a shallow dish that's large enough to hold the salmon and set aside to cool to room temperature.

About 2 hours before serving the salmon, prepare a sizable charcoal fire in a kettle grill, mounding the briquettes to cover two-thirds of the kettle's bottom grate.

As soon as you've prepared the charcoal, place the salmon, flesh side down, in the cooled brine. Let sit uncovered at room temperature for 1 hour. When the charcoal is ready (it will be mostly gray, and the flames will have subsided), remove the salmon from the brine and affix it to the plank, skin side down, with 8 nongalvanized, noncoated nails, spacing them so that they're not at the very edges of the fish, where they could pull out as the fish cooks. Tap the nails in only enough to secure the fish; you'll want to be able to remove them with pliers once the fish is cooked.

Carefully position the plank at an upright angle, approaching 90 degrees, on the open space on the grill's bottom grate, facing the hot charcoal. We place a brick next to the charcoal to keep the plank upright and to maintain a distance of 4 inches from the coals. As the fish cooks, keep an eye on the fire, which should be steady, not blazing—you want smoke and a low flame. Too much smoke will make the fish taste acrid, while too much flame will blacken it.

Keep watch, making sure that the plank doesn't slip or begin to catch fire at the bottom. (We keep a squeeze bottle full of water handy. You could use a laundry spritzer too, or simply a bowl with water.) You'll probably need to add 3 or 4 chunks of wood or additional charcoal to keep the fire going as the coals burn down, and you'll likely need to repeat this step once more before the fish is done.

After 25 minutes, rotate the plank 180 degrees, so that both parts of the fish will caramelize as the fat melts. If you're using a whole side of salmon, the middle section may not caramelize, but that's not a problem. For more even cooking, if necessary, you can rotate the plank a second time as the fish roasts. The total cooking time should be 45 to 60 minutes, depending on the heat of the fire.

Remove the plank from the fire, and with pliers, pull out the nails. Transfer the salmon to a large platter and serve by cutting crosswise into slices or chunks.

THIS DISH IS Norwegian fancy fare. Until New Nordic began making waves, upscale Scandinavian menus were inspired by French cuisine, and local chefs excelled in classical preparations. As the focus shifted to indigenous processes and ingredients, tastes changed, but Scandinavians still harbor a love for creamy dishes, especially for company or special occasions. This recipe is a case in point. It originated at the legendary restaurant Maison Troisgros in Roanne, France, with narrow strips of salmon and sturgeon caviar. This version comes from Norwegian chef Lars Barmen via my friend Helge Semb, who told me I absolutely had to try it. And so I did, adapting it for whole fillets. But then I hesitated, debating with myself whether or not to include it in this book. My head said no—after all, it's basically fish with a French *beurre blanc* and not aligned with the book's other recipes. But my heart—and my stomach—said yes. It's just too delicious not to share.

Ørretfilet med ørretrognsaus

TROUT FILLETS
WITH BEURRE BLANC, TROUT ROE, AND CHIVES

SERVES 2

2 whole trout (about 1 pound), cleaned, scaled, and gutted

Salt

2 shallots, finely chopped

4 tablespoons plus 1 teaspoon cold butter, cut into small pieces

½ cup dry white wine

½ cup heavy cream

2 tablespoons finely chopped fresh chives

Freshly ground white pepper

2 teaspoons canola oil

2 tablespoons trout roe

Remove the head, tail, and fins from the trout. Cut each fish in half lengthwise to yield 4 fillets. Lift out the backbone, sprinkle with salt, and set aside.

In a frying pan over medium-low heat, sauté the shallots in 1 tablespoon of the butter until they are soft but not brown, about 3 minutes. Raise the heat to medium, add the wine, and boil until most of the liquid has evaporated. Then add the cream and bring to a boil. Gradually whisk in 3 tablespoons of the butter until a sauce forms. Remove from the heat and stir in the chives. Season with salt and freshly ground white pepper to taste.

Heat the canola oil and the remaining 1 teaspoon of butter in a frying pan. Add the fillets, skin side down, and fry them for 3 minutes over medium-high heat. Lower the heat to medium, then flip the fillets. Insert a sharp fillet knife just under the skin and quickly remove the skin by pulling it away from the flesh. Cook for just 1 minute more—the surface that was under the skin should remain barely cooked. Place the fillets on a serving platter, fried side up. Spoon the sauce around them and garnish with the trout roe. Serve immediately.

NOTE: The recipe can easily be increased proportionally for more people—just use a larger frying pan for making the sauce and extra frying pans for cooking the trout.

cod

NORWAY MAY BE the largest petroleum producer in Europe, but in many ways the country's identity remains tied to a single fish, cod. Until wet-fish and factory trawlers began to proliferate in the 1980s, small-boat fishing was an economic mainstay and a way of life. This fishing culture was especially important to the Lofoten Islands, whose beaches are still lined with massive wooden drying racks, like so many geometric sculptures. When I first visited the Lofotens in 1981, I arrived on the Hurtigruten, a small ferry that plied the waters from Bergen to Kirkenes, like a maritime stagecoach delivering people, cargo, and mail to the isolated fishing communities along the coast.

Cod has been crucial for centuries, traded by the Vikings as early as the tenth century. Stockfish—dried cod—may have been Norway's first export. The cod is dried in various traditional ways, two of them recognized by Slow Food's Ark of Taste. These methods include the preparation of *tørrfisk* (stockfish) on Sørøya Island in the Norwegian Sea, where the cod is line-caught and quickly gutted and beheaded before being brought to shore. Two very fresh fish of similar size are then bound together by their tails and hung on wooden racks to dry for two or three months in the salt air. *Klippfisk* (salt cod) is a specialty of the region called Møre og Romsdal, farther south on Norway's west coast, where large, flat rocks (*klipper*) rise at the edge of the sea. The rocks are cleaned and spread with salt before laying split cod out on them to dry into a delicacy less brittle and hard than *tørrfisk*. Since the 1950s, special wind tunnels have been used for drying to create a more consistent product.

Locals revere all parts of the cod, including the cheeks, tongue, liver, and roe. The roe is lightly cured with sugar and salt, or mixed fresh with boiled potatoes for savory roe cakes. An old fishermen's one-pot meal is *mølje*, made by gently boiling the codfish, liver, and roe, with a little vinegar or whey added for piquancy. The dish is served over potatoes. Because cod liver is so high in vitamin D, frequent servings of *mølje* kept fishermen healthy during the long, sun-deprived winters. *Mølje*, like other nearly forgotten foods, has become fashionable again.

The cod that defined Norway's fisheries migrates from the Barents Sea, which washes both Norway and Russia. This sea is now home to the world's largest remaining population of wild cod, or *skrei*. These young cod—their Old Norse name means "to wander"—are distinct from the coastal cod known as *torsk*. They acquire exceptional flavor in the cold, nutrient-rich waters of the Barents, where they mature for five years before migrating to the west coast to spawn. From January to April they favor the Gulf Stream–warmed Lofotens, whose population once lived by the annual rhythms of breeding, migration, spawning, and fishing. But life is changing. After years of negotiation, Norway and Russia finally ratified the Barents Sea and Arctic Ocean Maritime Delimitation Treaty in 2010, opening up the waters to commercial interests. Although Norway is sensitive to environmental concerns, the country also feels pressure to drill for oil and natural gas in one of the last truly pristine places left on the globe.

Other changes similarly point to a less fishing-dependent way of life. In 2007 a road was completed to the Lofoten Islands, turning them into an easy tourist destination. The islands' thousands of cod-drying racks stand as decorative reminders of a fading past. The Hurtigruten, the beloved mail boat, has been replaced with a deluxe cruise ship, enclosed with glass and offering plenty of bars to keep passengers occupied as it purrs up the coast. But its comforts also serve to isolate the passengers, distancing them from the elements, from the sea, from fishing as a way of life.

MEAT + POULTRY

The Nordic appreciation for pork is legendary: the gods in Valhalla, the Norse paradise, are believed to have feasted on boiled and roasted boar. A 2010 survey counted 2.3 pigs per person in Denmark, making that country more porcine even than China, the world's largest producer of pork.

Lamb is also greatly enjoyed. Sheep roam the Nordic landscape, vying with goats for the title of most picturesque. Their meat finds its way into delicious dill-infused stews and hearty braises with beer. Lamb is sometimes still prepared in the manner of mutton, which had to be tenderized in a marinade of buttermilk or whey before roasting. Beef is eaten more frequently today than it was in the past, especially in Sweden, where Biff à la Lindström—hamburgers studded with pickled beets and capers (see page 172)—is a contemporary classic. Of course, all manner of ground meat—pork, lamb, beef, and veal—go into much-loved Nordic meatballs, typically flavored with allspice or cloves.

Reindeer once roamed wild in the Arctic regions of Finland, Norway, and Sweden. The nomadic Sami people, whose traditional livelihood depended on the reindeer, domesticated them several centuries ago, and today reindeer meat is a widely available delicacy, eaten fresh, smoked, and cured.

Game in any form, especially wildfowl, is considered a treat in Scandinavia, and the opening of hunting season in early September is marked by celebration. For those who don't hunt, urban purveyors create gorgeous displays of wild birds, from capercaillie and black grouse to pheasant and ptarmigan, their kaleidoscopic plumage luring shoppers to the meat counter. Once in the kitchen, even the lean meat of pheasant turns moist and succulent when braised with bacon, onions, white cabbage, and juniper berries that echo the bird's wild habitat. Beginning in late autumn, and especially at Christmas, roasted farm-raised fowl appear on the table, especially goose and duck, whose rich, dark flesh gets treated to a sweet and sour stuffing.

THIS BEAUTIFUL AUTUMNAL dish can be made in under an hour. The quick cooking ensures a moist bird and cabbage with just the right amount of bite. Although most of the pheasant available in the States is farm raised, it still has a slightly wild flavor that I like to accentuate with juniper berries.

Brasiert fasan med einer og kål

 # BRAISED PHEASANT
WITH JUNIPER AND CABBAGE

SERVES 4

4 thick slices bacon, coarsely chopped

1 yellow onion, chopped

1 pheasant hen (2¼ pounds)

Salt and freshly ground pepper

1 cup chicken stock

1 small head white cabbage (2 pounds), cored and cut into 8 to 10 wedges

2 sprigs thyme

8 juniper berries

3 allspice berries

Preheat the oven to 350°F. In a 4-quart braising pan with a lid, sauté the bacon and onion over medium heat until the onions are soft but not brown, about 10 minutes.

Rub the pheasant all over with salt and pepper. Place it in the pan with the bacon and onions and sear it until brown, about 5 minutes on each side. With a spatula or slotted spoon, transfer the pheasant to a plate, along with the bacon and onions.

Pour off most of the fat in the pan, then deglaze it with a little of the stock, scraping up any browned bits stuck to the bottom of the pan. Pour in the remaining stock and add the cabbage to the pan, along with the thyme, juniper, and allspice. Cover the pan and simmer over low heat until the cabbage begins to soften, about 10 minutes. Return the pheasant to the pan, breast side up, along with the bacon and onion. Cover the pan tightly with the lid and bake until the meat is cooked through, about 30 minutes.

If you like the skin crisp and brown, set the pheasant under the broiler for a minute or two just before serving.

THIS BEAUTIFUL STEW, a Swedish classic, comes from Jens Linder, a Stockholm food writer who makes magic in the kitchen. Many versions of *dillkött* are sharply sweet and sour, but Jens likes his mild, and he's on to something. Even Anthony Bourdain, that seeker of gustatory sensation, had three servings when Jens offered this stew during an interview.

Without the heavy cream, *dillkött* is elegant and delicate, but cream turns it lush and soul satisfying. For a more intense dill flavor, you can add ¼ teaspoon of dill seed. Either way, this stew is a breeze to prepare.

Dillkött

VEAL STEW
WITH DILL
SERVES 4

1½ pounds veal stew meat, cut into 1½-inch cubes

2 cups water

¾ teaspoon salt

1 carrot, peeled and cut into ½-inch slices

1 small leek, white part only, cleaned and cut into ½-inch slices

5 white peppercorns

½ cup coarsely chopped dill stems

1 tablespoon butter

1 tablespoon flour

1 teaspoon freshly squeezed lemon juice

1 teaspoon sugar

¼ cup finely chopped dill fronds

Freshly ground white pepper

Boiled potatoes, for serving

Place the meat in a 2-quart pot. Bring the water and salt to a boil in another pot and pour it over the meat. Bring the water to a boil again, skimming any scum that rises to the surface.

Add the carrot, leek, peppercorns, and dill stems. Cover, lower the heat, and simmer until the meat is very tender, about 1¼ hours. Strain the broth, reserving the meat but discarding the vegetables. Measure out 1 cup of the broth. Save any remaining broth for another use.

In a stockpot, melt the butter over low heat and add the flour, stirring constantly until the mixture sizzles, a few minutes. Slowly pour in the 1 cup of broth, whisking constantly. Simmer briefly until the sauce thickens, then add the meat and simmer until it is heated through, about 5 minutes more.

Add the lemon juice, sugar, and dill fronds. Season with white pepper to taste. Serve immediately, with boiled potatoes.

VARIATIONS: For a richer stew, combine 1 small egg yolk with ½ cup of heavy cream and slowly stir into the stew, heating only until the sauce thickens. Do not let boil. Season with salt and white pepper.

Substitute boneless lamb for the veal. This version is most often found in Finland, where it is known as *tilliliha*.

AFTER COOKING IN Gothenburg for a decade, chef Michael Björklund returned to his native Åland Islands to open Smakbyn, a gorgeous restaurant that showcases the foods of Åland and the Nordic region with a menu inspired by home cooking rather than modernist technique. Though Michael's food is all about eating locally, he's ultimately more interested in living in harmony with the seasons and the environment and allowing those forces to drive his creativity. Besides preserving all sorts of indigenous plants like sea buckthorn, he smokes his own fish and distills brandy from the famed Åland apples, cleverly named Ålvados.

These short ribs are inspired by one of Michael's recipes from the cookbook *Mat så in i Norden* (*Food from the Nordic Lands*). While Michael suggests braising lamb shanks in mead or wheat beer, I prefer using more manageable short ribs, since American lamb shanks tend to be enormous. I add honey to recall the flavor of mead. The ribs cook up meltingly tender, with the perfect degree of sweetness. Serve them with potatoes or steamed barley.

Honungs- och ölbräserade revben av nöt

HONEY- AND BEER-BRAISED SHORT RIBS
WITH ROOT VEGETABLES

SERVES 4 TO 6

2 tablespoons vegetable oil

4 pounds bone-in beef short ribs, cut into 3-inch pieces

Salt and freshly ground pepper

1 large head garlic

3 yellow onions, coarsely chopped

3 carrots, peeled and coarsely chopped

3 sprigs thyme

2 large sprigs parsley, and 2 tablespoons minced parsley

½ cup honey

1 (12-ounce) bottle wheat ale

Preheat the oven to 300°F. Heat the oil in a 6-quart braising pan with a lid over medium heat. Rub the short ribs all over with salt and pepper. Place them in the pan and sear until brown, about 2 minutes on each side. With tongs, transfer the short ribs to a plate and pour off all of the fat from the pan.

Remove the outer papery skin from the head of garlic and cut about ½ inch off the top to reveal the cloves.

Return the short ribs to the pan and nestle the head of garlic, cut side up, among them. Strew the onions and carrots among the meat, and stick the thyme and parsley sprigs into any nooks.

Whisk together the honey and beer in a bowl and pour the mixture over the meat and vegetables (it won't cover them). Cover the pan tightly with the lid and bake for 2 hours.

CONTINUED

HONEY- AND BEER-BRAISED SHORT RIBS
WITH ROOT VEGETABLES
CONTINUED

Raise the oven temperature to 400°F and continue to bake the meat until it is very tender and the liquid has turned slightly syrupy, about 45 minutes more.

Blot or skim off as much fat as you can. I like to serve the ribs home-style, right from the pan, but you can also transfer the meat and vegetables to a deep serving bowl. Garnish with the minced parsley and serve hot.

NOTE: Since short ribs are fatty, I like to make this dish the day before and let it cool to room temperature, then refrigerate it overnight. The next day you can easily lift off all of the fat that has risen to the surface. Reheat the stew gently at 300°F for an hour or so.

STUDDED WITH SHALLOTS, capers, and eggs, these succulent hamburgers taste like a cooked version of steak tartare, though their pickled beets and beet brine hint at a different origin. The story goes that the dish Biff à la Lindström was named for the industrialist Henrik Lindström, who was born in Saint Petersburg, Russia, to a Swedish family. In 1862 Lindström visited the city of Kalmar, on Sweden's southeast Baltic coast, where he stayed, and of course dined, at the elegant Hotel Witt. On the night of May 4 he wanted to share a Russian-style dish with his friends, so he asked the chef to bring out freshly minced beef, onions, capers, pickled beets, and raw eggs, which he mixed right at the table. He then directed the chef to shape the mixture into patties and fry them. The dish became a Swedish classic that bears his name. And 150 years later, it's still on the menu at Hotel Witt's Lindström Bar & Bistro.

Biff à la Lindström

SAVORY BEEF PATTIES

SERVES 4

3 tablespoons butter

3 tablespoons minced shallot

1 pound ground beef

3 egg yolks

2 tablespoons capers, drained and finely chopped

¼ cup finely chopped pickled beets

2 tablespoons pickled beet brine

1 teaspoon salt

Freshly ground pepper

1 tablespoon vegetable oil

Diced pickled beets, for garnish

Capers, for garnish

Minced fresh parsley or chives, for garnish

Melt 1 tablespoon of the butter in a large skillet over medium-low heat, add the shallot, and sauté until golden, about 4 minutes.

In a large bowl, stir together the beef with the cooked shallot, egg yolks, capers, beets, beet brine, salt, and a generous amount of pepper. The mixture should be moist but hold together well. Let sit covered for 1 hour at room temperature or up to 8 hours in the refrigerator.

Shape the beef mixture into fourteen 2-inch patties. In the same skillet, melt the remaining 2 tablespoons of butter with the oil over medium heat. When the butter sizzles, add the patties and cook for 5 minutes. Flip and cook them on the other side until medium-rare, about 3 minutes more (it will be a little hard to tell when the meat is medium-rare since the beets and beet juice turn it red).

Transfer the patties to a platter and garnish with some diced pickled beets and capers and a little minced parsley or chives for color.

VARIATION: Make four 6-inch patties. Cook them over medium heat until medium-rare, about 5 minutes on each side. Top each patty with a fried sunny-side up egg that is still slightly runny in the center.

"SALT BEEF" SOUNDS like something packed in barrels for the British navy. In Swedish, it's more evocatively called "frost bump." Neither name does it justice. No matter what you call this dish, it's scrumptious and ideal for entertaining because you can prepare it well ahead of time, and it serves a crowd.

Tjälknöl comes from Norrland, in the Swedish North. Unlike other cured meats—corned beef comes to mind—it isn't brined for days before simmering. Instead, a hunk (a "bump") of frozen beef is put into a cold oven, where it is slow-cooked at an extremely low temperature for eight hours or more. Only then does it get a brief bath in brine. This method, which is traditionally used for game like elk, ensures that tough cuts of meat will be tender. It also yields a subtly salty taste. Serve the meat cold with horseradish cream (page 35) or lingonberry jam on the side. The traditional accompaniment is hot roasted or mashed root vegetables.

Tjälknöl
SLOW-ROASTED SALT BEEF

SERVES 10 TO 12

4 pounds bottom round of beef, including the rump, frozen

8 cups water

1 cup salt

2 teaspoons sugar

2 teaspoons juniper berries, crushed

3 large cloves garlic, crushed

1 teaspoon white peppercorns

1 teaspoon black peppercorns

2 bay leaves

Place the frozen meat, fat side up, in a baking dish or roasting pan with low sides in the lower third of a cold oven. Set the oven temperature to 175°F and roast the meat until an instant-read thermometer inserted into the thickest part registers 140°F, 8 to 9 hours.

While the meat is roasting, there is plenty of time to make the brine. In a large saucepan, bring the water, salt, sugar, juniper, garlic, peppercorns, and bay leaves to a boil until the salt and sugar dissolve. Turn off the heat and let the brine cool to room temperature in the pan. Transfer to a deep pot or bowl large enough to hold the roast.

When the meat is cooked, place the meat in the brine and refrigerate it, covered, for 5 hours. Remove the meat from the brine, rinse, and pat dry with paper towels. Slice very thinly, and serve cold or at room temperature.

NOTES: For ease of slicing, have the butcher tie the roast for you. I generally put the meat in the oven before I go to bed and check it first thing in the morning. The brine can be made ahead and left to cool overnight.

MY FRIEND EJA Nilsson grew up in Stockholm but has lived in Copenhagen for thirty-five years. When I asked her to name a favorite Danish food, she immediately mentioned *boller i selleri*. It's a dish of pure comfort. This stew couldn't be simpler: Just boil celery root to create a broth for cooking meatballs, which lend additional flavor to the sauce. Make a buttery roux to finish it, and voilà! You have a beautiful autumnal dish. Most Danish cooks add an onion to the meat mixture, but I prefer the subtler taste of shallot.

Boller i selleri

MEATBALL AND CELERY ROOT STEW

SERVES 4

5 cups water

Salt

1 celery root (about 1¾ pounds), peeled and cut into 1-inch chunks

8 ounces ground beef

8 ounces ground pork

1 shallot, minced

1 small egg, lightly beaten

Pinch of ground cloves

Freshly ground pepper

5 tablespoons flour

¼ cup whole milk

4 tablespoons unsalted butter

Boiled white rice, for serving

Bring the water to a boil in a wide 4-quart pan. Sprinkle in some salt and lower the heat. Add the celery root and cook gently, partly covered, until just tender, 8 to 10 minutes. Remove the celery root with a slotted spoon and set aside. Keep the celery root broth warm.

While the celery root is cooking, make the meatballs. In a bowl, mix together the beef, pork, shallot, egg, cloves, 1 teaspoon of salt, and a few grindings of pepper. Stir in 1 tablespoon of the flour and the milk. The meat mixture will be light and sticky.

Coat your hands lightly with vegetable oil and form the meat mixture into about 2 dozen 1-inch meatballs.

Bring the celery root broth to a boil and drop in the meatballs. Lower the heat and simmer, uncovered, until the meatballs have cooked through, about 15 minutes. With a slotted spoon, transfer the meatballs to a plate. Measure the remaining broth. You should have about 3 cups.

Rinse the pan. Melt the butter over low heat, then stir in the remaining 4 tablespoons of flour and cook until bubbly, about 1 minute. Slowly add the 3 cups of reserved broth, whisking constantly. Raise the heat to medium and let the broth boil briefly until slightly thickened.

Lower the heat, add the meatballs and celery root, and simmer, uncovered, about 10 minutes.

Serve over rice.

THIS MINIMALIST STEW is beloved by Finns. When Michelin-starred chef Sasu Laukkonen came to New York to give a master class, it was one of only three dishes he chose to demonstrate. It's perfectly simple to make, requiring no browning of meat and no added fat. Traditionally this stew was baked in a wood-fired oven after the fire had died down, as the heat declined—slow cooking at its best. I like to add juniper berries to recall that smoky taste. The flavors are beautiful in their simplicity but, to the modern palate, a little bland—which is why I recommend a generous garnish of garlicky dill pickles to perk the stew up. Serve this dish with boiled or mashed new potatoes and lingonberry jam. Beets are also a good accompaniment.

Karjalanpaisti

KARELIAN STEW

SERVES 4

3½ pounds bone-in or boneless stew meat (a mix of beef, lamb, and pork), cut into 2-inch cubes

1 tablespoon salt

2 yellow onions, each cut into 8 wedges

2 large carrots, peeled and cut into 1-inch lengths

6 allspice berries

12 black peppercorns

4 juniper berries (optional)

2 bay leaves

Water just to cover (about 3 cups)

Chopped dill pickles, for garnish

Preheat the oven to 400°F. Season the meat with the salt. Place a layer of the meat on the bottom of a 4-quart casserole, preferably enameled cast iron or earthenware. Top it with some of the onions and carrots, then sprinkle on some of the allspice, peppercorns, and juniper berries. Repeat the layers until all the ingredients have been used. Tuck in the bay leaves and pour the water over the top.

Cover the casserole and bake 20 minutes, then lower the heat to 275°F and bake until the meat is very tender and there's a flavorful broth, about 4 hours more.

Don't forget to top each serving with a generous garnish of pickles.

FINNS MAKE A kind of meat stew called *käristys* with all sorts of game–reindeer, venison, moose, even bear. The most traditional, *poronkäristys*, is a Sami dish from the Arctic made with reindeer, which is virtually impossible to find in the States. So I've substituted venison here, which can be ordered by mail (see Sources).

Maybe because of our sentimental attachment to Rudolph and his nose so bright, even I felt some guilt the first time I ate reindeer. We were living in Stockholm, and our playful English friends thought it would be funny to serve us "Saddle of Rudolph" for Christmas dinner. It was delicious. Reindeer is too tasty to ignore, and I've eaten it many times since then–smoked, roasted, thinly sliced as carpaccio, or in *suovas*, a Sami dish of salted and smoked reindeer that has been inducted into the Slow Food Ark of Taste.

The Sami herders make the original dish very simply: after melting fat in a cauldron, they shave in thin slices of frozen meat, add a little snow for moisture, and let the stew bubble. Because reindeer are their livelihood, they honor the meat by letting its flavor shine through, with little seasoning. This modern version remains simple, although butter, onion, and plenty of black pepper enrich the dish, which despite its minimal ingredients is anything but bland. Mashed potatoes–another modern innovation– soak up the flavorful broth, and a little lingonberry jam adds a lively touch.

Poronkäristys

 # VENISON STEW

SERVES 4

1¾ pounds frozen venison (loin or steak)

8 tablespoons (1 stick) butter

2 teaspoons salt

½ teaspoon freshly ground pepper

1 large yellow onion, chopped

1¼ to 1½ cups water

Mashed potatoes, for serving

Lingonberry jam, for serving

Allow the meat to thaw slightly so that it can be handled with greater ease, about 20 minutes. It should remain frozen but not be rock-solid. Using a very sharp knife or an electric meat slicer, shave the meat into wafer-thin slices. I'm lucky to have an expert knife wielder in my husband, but if you find that the meat is still highly frozen, or if your knife skills are less than perfect, it's a good idea, once you have a pile of shaved meat, to put it in the freezer as you continue to work, so that it doesn't thaw.

Melt the butter in a 12-inch cast-iron skillet over medium-low heat. When the butter sizzles, add the meat all at once. Cook it, stirring occasionally, over high heat until brown, 6 to 8 minutes.

Season with the salt and pepper. Stir in the onion and just enough water to barely cover the meat. Lower the heat and simmer, covered, for 30 minutes. Serve with mashed potatoes and lingonberry jam.

CHRISTMAS IN AUGUST was the theme of a beautiful dinner we had at Bodil and Harry Wilson's Berkshires house. Bodil prepared the special dishes she has made for Christmas Eve for half a century now: roast duck with fruits, caramelized potatoes (page 206), and sweet and sour red cabbage (page 208). She even brought out an embroidered table runner and decorated the house with *julenisser*–Christmas elves. Although the summer sun was still bright at 8 p.m., we closed the drapes, and the atmosphere turned so warming that we could imagine ourselves on a dark, wintry night. And sure enough, at the end of the meal, we opened the curtains to a starry sky. It was a lovely celebration, filled with earthy flavors and aromas and good cheer.

I've played with Bodil's recipe a little bit, using apple cider instead of water as the duck roasts to feature the apples so distinctive of Danish cuisine–and of the Berkshires. The prunes will make the filling sweeter; how many you choose to use will depend on the desired balance between sweet and sour.

Andesteg med æbler og svesker

ROAST DUCK
WITH APPLES AND PRUNES

SERVES 4

1 (6-pound) duck

Salt

½ lemon

3 firm apples, peeled and cut into 8 wedges

15 to 20 prunes

Freshly ground pepper

2 cups apple cider

2 teaspoons flour

Preheat the oven to 400°F. Remove the extra fat from the duck, along with the neck and gizzard. Cut off the wing tips.

Rub the inside of the duck with salt and then with the lemon, squeezing the juice out into the cavity. Stuff the duck at both ends with the apples and prunes. Either sew the cavities shut with kitchen twine or close them with trussing skewers.

Rub the outside of the duck generously with salt and pepper. Place the duck on a rack in a roasting pan, breast side down. Roast for 10 minutes, then turn the duck breast side up and roast for another 10 minutes. Duck has a lot of fat, and the high heat allows much of it to cook off.

Lower the oven to 300°F. Remove the duck from the oven and pour the cider into the roasting pan. Roast the duck until the juices run rosy when the meat is pricked, about 1¾ hours.

CONTINUED

ROAST DUCK WITH APPLES AND PRUNES
CONTINUED

Raise the oven to 450°F and roast the duck for 10 minutes more to crisp the skin. Transfer the duck to a carving board. Let the duck rest for 10 minutes before carving.

While the duck is resting, make the gravy. Pour the pan juices into a fat separator to remove the fat. You should have about 1 cup of defatted pan juices. Place the roasting pan on a burner and deglaze it with a little water, scraping up any browned bits stuck to the bottom of the pan. Pour about three-fourths of the pan juices into the roasting pan, reserving the rest.

Place the flour in a small bowl and gradually add a little of the reserved pan juices, whisking constantly to avoid lumps. Add the remaining reserved pan juices, then whisk this mixture into the juices in the roasting pan. Cook the gravy over medium-low heat until it has thickened, a few minutes.

With a large spoon, scoop the apples and prunes out of the duck and transfer to a serving bowl. Carve the duck into thin slices and place them on a platter. Serve with the fruit stuffing and a pitcher of the gravy.

NORWEGIANS TENDERIZED LAMB with the whey left over from cheese making, or the buttermilk left in the bottom of the butter churn. Old recipes call for soaking the meat in a cool place for six days, but I've found that three days in the refrigerator works just fine. In classic preparations, this parsley-studded lamb roast is served with a sour cream sauce, but I recommend it plain, to let the pure tastes of the lamb and parsley shine through.

Lammelår i surmelk med persille

BUTTERMILK-MARINATED LEG OF LAMB
WITH PARSLEY
SERVES 4 TO 6

1 (4-pound) bone-in leg of lamb

4 cups buttermilk

1 cup finely chopped parsley

2 teaspoons salt

Freshly ground pepper

In a large, shallow, nonreactive dish, soak the lamb in buttermilk for 3 days in the refrigerator, covered with plastic wrap, turning occasionally. A few hours before serving, take the lamb out of the refrigerator to bring it to room temperature. Remove from the buttermilk and pat dry with paper towels.

Stir together the parsley and salt in a small bowl. With a sharp knife, make small slits all over the meaty parts of the lamb to create rather deep pockets. Stuff them with the salted parsley mixture. Rub the lamb all over with pepper.

Preheat the oven to 450°F. Place the lamb on a rack in a roasting pan, fat side up, and roast until it registers 135°F for medium-rare, 30 to 35 minutes.

Let the lamb rest for 10 minutes before carving into thick slices.

NOTE: I love the seasonally available Icelandic leg of lamb, which is small and tender, with a subtle taste. If you use a more standard semi-boned 6-pound leg of lamb, you'll need 8 cups of buttermilk for the marinade. Increase the amount of parsley to 1½ cups and the salt to 1 tablespoon. With this larger cut, the meat will take approximately 1 hour to reach the proper temperature.

CABBAGE TOO OFTEN gets a bad rap in the States. Maybe it's the smell when the vegetable boils, or the memory of too many picnic bowls filled with overly vinegary slaw. But it doesn't have to be that way.

One of Sweden's most beloved cabbage dishes is *kåldolmar* or dolma—stuffed cabbage leaves—whose name betrays their Eastern Mediterranean origin. Dolma arrived rather circuitously in Sweden in the early eighteenth century, courtesy of Sweden's humiliating war with Russia. After his defeat at the Battle of Poltava, King Karl XII fled to Turkey. That much is historically certain. But here accounts diverge. Some say the king fell in love with Ottoman food and ordered his cooks to prepare dolma after he returned to Sweden, substituting cabbage for grape leaves. Others say he was hounded by Turkish creditors carrying with them a taste for dolma. Whatever the true story, it's a known fact that Swedes came to love these meat-filled bundles. They're now a regular feature of the *smörgåsbord*, often served with a brown sauce and accompanied by boiled potatoes and lingonberry jam, which offsets their sweetness.

Kåldolmar

STUFFED CABBAGE ROLLS

SERVES 4

1 cup plus 2 tablespoons vegetable broth

3 tablespoons rice

1 small head white cabbage (about 2 pounds)

1 small yellow onion, finely chopped

1 tablespoon butter

12 ounces ground meat (beef, veal, or pork, or a combination)

1 large egg, lightly beaten

2 tablespoons minced fresh dill or parsley

1 tablespoon heavy cream

1 teaspoon salt

Freshly ground pepper

2 tablespoons cane syrup or unsulphured molasses

1 cup apple cider

2 to 3 teaspoons cornstarch

Minced fresh dill or parsley, for garnish

To make the rice, bring ½ cup of the broth to a boil in a small saucepan. Stir in the rice, then lower the heat and simmer, covered, until the liquid has been absorbed, about 15 minutes. Remove from the heat and set aside.

To prepare the cabbage, bring a large pot of salted water to a boil. Core the cabbage and then blanch it in the boiling water for about 5 minutes. Remove from the pot with a large slotted spoon and gently peel off the outer leaves. If the inner leaves are still too stiff to be peeled, return the cabbage to the boiling water for another few minutes. Continue until all the leaves have been removed. Set aside the 15 to 16 nicest leaves, including the largest, outer ones. Reserve the remaining leaves.

In a small skillet over medium-low heat, sauté the onion in the butter until just soft and slightly golden, 5 to 7 minutes. In a small bowl, stir together the meat, cooked onion, cooked rice, egg, dill, cream, and salt. Season with pepper. The mixture should be moist.

CONTINUED

STUFFED CABBAGE ROLLS
CONTINUED

Place a cabbage leaf on a cutting board so that the "cup" side is up and trim any hard spots near the core end, for ease of rolling. Divide the filling mixture into 15 to 16 portions, depending on how many cabbage leaves you have.

To assemble a cabbage roll, place a mound of the filling along the center of the leaf. Tuck up the cored end, fold in one side, then roll and tuck in the other side of the leaf until the filling is completely enclosed. Repeat until all of the filling has been used.

Preheat the oven to 400°F. Butter a deep, 2-quart ovenproof casserole with a lid and line the bottom with the reserved cabbage leaves; broken ones are fine. Place half of the cabbage rolls, seam side down, in a single layer on top of the cabbage leaves.

Drizzle with 1 tablespoon of the cane syrup, using your finger or a brush to spread it evenly over the tops of the cabbage rolls. Layer the remaining cabbage rolls on top and drizzle with the remaining 1 tablespoon cane syrup.

Bake the cabbage rolls, covered, for 20 minutes. While the cabbage rolls are baking, in a glass measuring cup, stir together the cider and the remaining broth. Lower the heat to 350°F and remove the casserole from the oven. Pour the cider mixture over the cabbage rolls to cover. If there isn't quite enough liquid to cover the rolls due to the shape of your pan, it's fine to add a little more broth. Bake, uncovered, until the liquid bubbles and the tops of the cabbage rolls are lightly browned, about 45 minutes more, basting the rolls once about halfway through the cooking.

Carefully transfer the cabbage rolls to a serving dish; keep warm by tenting them with foil.

Remove the extra cabbage leaves from the bottom of the casserole and pour the cooking liquid into a measuring cup. You should have 1 to 1½ cups of cooking liquid. For each 1 cup of cooking liquid, you'll need 2 teaspoons of cornstarch. Transfer the cooking liquid to a saucepan and bring to a boil. Measure out the amount of cornstarch needed and place in a small bowl. Add a couple of tablespoons of hot broth to the cornstarch, whisking well to remove any lumps. Then pour the cornstarch mixture into the cooking liquid in the pan and bring to a boil. Lower the heat and simmer until the sauce thickens, just a minute, then pour over the cabbage rolls. Serve liberally garnished with dill or parsley.

NOTE: If you can only find a large head of cabbage, blanching the leaves will take longer, so plan accordingly.

NORWAY

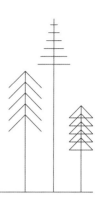

People look at the calendar differently in Norway, where each week's number tells them how many hours of daylight to expect. When my friend Bendik invited me to sail north of the Arctic Circle during week 46, in mid-November, he knew to the minute when the sun would set. At the North Cape, only ten days remained before total darkness would descend.

I'd been to the north of Norway before, in midsummer, years earlier when my husband and I took the Hurtigruten, the old mail boat, down the coast, hopscotching from Narvik south to Bergen. Though the air was chill, the days were gloriously unending. Talking on the phone with Bendik, I tried to imagine Norway's November winterscape. I pictured the small mail packet floundering in rough waters, precariously close to the maelstrom—the stuff of childhood terror— swirling south of the Lofoten Islands. Long before Edgar Allan Poe turned his gaze on the Norwegian Sea's shifting eddies, the sixteenth-century historian Olaus Magnus described Scandinavia as a land of *mirabilia*, filled with geysers, volcanoes, and maelstroms, writing that "those who sail at the wrong time are suddenly snatched down into spiraling abysses." Gulp! Edvard Munch's painting *The Scream* suddenly lurched into view. And then I saw trolls and the invisible *huldrefolk* who live underground and make mischief.

But soon enough I came to my senses. The Norway of the past was wilder, scarier, and more folkloric. Today Norway is one of the richest countries in the world, modern and troll-free. So I packed my heavy parka and boots and set off for my far northern adventure. I needn't have worried. The new Hurtigruten is no little ferry but a sleek luxury liner, with several floors of restaurants, cinemas, conference rooms, and bars that serve up more varieties of *akvavit* than I knew existed. The cruise from Tromsø to Kirkenes, near the border with Russia, lasted three days, with a stop at the North Cape, where the Norwegian and Barents Seas meet; the Atlantic and the Arctic. What a joy to step off the boat, to feel the Arctic wind in my face and snow swirling all around! Back onboard I warmed myself with shots of *akvavit* and surprisingly delectable slices of *Westfjordschinke*, "West Fjord ham," whale meat cured in the style of prosciutto.

Norway is long and skinny, with 64,000 miles of coastline, if you include its islands, and nearly 1,200 fjords—deep, dramatic inlets bounded by steep, rocky cliffs. This topography of mountains and fjords has defined Norway as a place of isolation, one in which socializing was dependent on village life, especially during the snow-covered months. Because only about 3 percent of the land is arable, Norway became a land of fishermen. Yet most of the catch was destined for export, and even along the coast the bulk of the population survived on porridge, flatbread, and dairy. Whatever fish, meat, and game was eaten was, like the breads and dairy products, creatively processed to last for months, through fermentation, brining, salting, smoking, or drying.

This diet may have been monotonous, but it wasn't bland. The Norwegian palate is marked by a preference for strong flavors, what Food Network adventurers might call "extreme." These include the well-known lye-cured lutefisk, the butt of many jokes, as well as the fermented trout known as *rakefisk*, a pungent accompaniment to *akvavit* and beer. An even more extraordinary form of preserved fish is *rødsaithe* (red saithe), made from a type of pollock layered with salt in a barrel and left to ripen for one to four years (hence its alternate name of "old saithe"). Because the fish's blood has bacteriostatic properties that counteract spoilage, the fish isn't bled before salting. Once removed from the brine, the saithe is soaked to draw out excess salt, then boiled and served with carrots or rutabaga, bringing beautiful color to the table—a white fish metamorphosed into red.

Red saithe has its counterpart in *gamalost* (literally "old cheese"), a stinky, fermented cheese that today carries Protected Geographical Indication status. Made from buttermilk or soured milk, it has been dubbed the "Viking Viagra"—those virile men allegedly used it not only to heal their wounds but also to enhance their sexual prowess. Ironically, perhaps, *gamalost* is now produced by the same dairy

that introduced Jarlsberg, that most mild of cheeses, in the late 1950s. No one makes claims for Jarlsberg's aphrodisiac properties.

Other Norwegian dairy products that ask us to acclimate our palates include the ancient and healthy drink *blanda*, a mixture of water and whey, which old-timers still like to imbibe. And then there's *brunost*, or brown cheese, the generic name given to a whole range of cheeses made by cooking whey over low heat for several hours until it caramelizes and turns deep golden in color and somewhat sticky in texture. *Brunost* caught the world's attention in 2013 when a truck carrying the stuff crashed above the Arctic Circle, near Narvik. The high proportion of milk sugar in the cheese caused it to go up in flames, and the fire burned for four days, blocking access to the road's single tunnel. The favorite form of *brunost* in Norway, approaching a national passion, is *geitost*, made from goat's milk whey, milk, and cream (sometimes the goat's milk is mixed with cow's milk). It is salty-sweet, and nearly as rich as fudge. An even stronger variety is *ekte geitost* (genuine goat's whey cheese), made solely from goat products that yield a deeper flavor and color. Seasonal *brunost* for Christmas becomes even sweeter with the addition of sugar and cardamom.

The Norwegian taste for rich dairy products is reflected in *rømmegrøt*, an old-fashioned sour cream porridge still beloved, though the younger generation shies away from this kind of caloric fare. Pure sour cream (without stabilizers or gelatin) is gently boiled until it liquefies. At that point some flour is stirred in and the mixture continues to boil until the cream's butterfat rises to the surface. This golden prize is skimmed off and set aside before the rest of the flour is added, along with some milk. The mixture is then boiled down into porridge, served with the reserved butterfat gilding the top and with a sprinkling of sugar and cinnamon. The traditional accompaniment is something pungent and salty, like cured ham, fermented fish, or *surstek*, meat that has marinated for several days in whey or buttermilk before cooking. In earlier eras *rømmegrøt* was considered an appropriate wedding or housewarming gift and was regularly offered to women who had just given birth, because it's so nutritious. Special lidded containers for presenting the porridge were decorated with brightly painted designs or carvings.

Norway had its share of Viking settlements, but the people living along the country's remote northern coast also engaged in lively barter with inhabitants of Russia's Far North. This Pomor trade, named after the Russian word for "coastal," flourished from the mid-eighteenth century until the Russian Revolution in 1917 shut down all cross-border contact, causing hardship on both sides. The Pomor trade had been important to the marginal economies of both countries' northernmost peoples, and even gave birth to a distinctive pidgin language called Russenorsk. Northern Norway relied on Russian grain during lean harvests, while the Russians looked to Norway's rich fisheries for the massive amounts of fish needed to properly observe the Orthodox Church's many fast days.

Although the Pomor trade and its quirky language died out, an unexpected kind of migration ensued across the Barents Sea. In the 1930s Stalin decided to try to appease the populace by making delectable Kamchatka (red king) crab accessible to the lowliest of workers. His plan was to transport this giant crustacean—whose leg span can reach up to six feet in length—from Russia's Far East, where it thrived in the Bering Sea, to the Barents Sea, to feed European Russia. These early attempts failed, but the Soviets kept at it and finally, in the 1960s, biologists succeeded in establishing a crab colony in the Kola Fjord. The subsequent story of the Kamchatka crab shows the limits of totalitarianism in a region defined by a common geography. Unhappy under Soviet rule, the crabs fled northwest into Norwegian waters. The Norwegians have been struggling ever since to rout these voracious crustaceans and restore ecological balance.

Until the boom in oil and natural gas production of the 1970s transformed the country's economy, Norway had been the poorest of the Scandinavian sisters, first under the thumb of Denmark (a period Henrik Ibsen called "the four hundred–year night") and then under Swedish rule. Norway didn't gain independence until May 17, 1905, a date still fiercely celebrated today. But old impressions die hard. Thanks to Norway's image as a hardscrabble place, many Swedes and Danes continue to dismiss the country's food as uninteresting and bland. (This attitude may partly be due to sibling rivalry, now that Norway's oil wealth has made the country so affluent.) Though they concede that the country's chefs are among the best in the world (the Norwegian team regularly wins in the Bocuse d'Or culinary competition), other Scandinavians paid little attention until recently to Norway's exquisite raw ingredients. These include not only the abundant sea fish—especially the cod, saithe, halibut, herring, and mackerel—but also the river and lake fish like salmon, arctic char, and trout. The wild grasses and herbs of the alpine pastures lend

extraordinary flavor to Norwegian lamb, which is roasted or delicately cured into prosciutto-like *fenalår*. The meat also finds its way into *får-i-kål*, an autumnal stew of lamb or mutton with cabbage that marks the end of summer pasturing. Embellished only with salt and black pepper, the stew allows the herbaceous flavor of the lamb to shine through. Just as cinnamon buns have their day in Sweden, so does *får-i-kål* in Norway, on the last Thursday of September.

Autumn also signals the opening of hunting season. The North abounds in wildfowl like wood grouse, black grouse, and ptarmigan. Moose is a favorite meat, especially when braised in strong, dark beer with onions and mountain thyme, and a sauce finished with cream; moose is also ground into burgers scented with crushed juniper berries. Reindeer is cooked into minimalist stews or simply roasted, or the fillet can be air-dried like cod for a lovely Nordic bresaola.

Christmas is marked with special dishes. These include lutefisk, pork ribs with loin (*ribbe*), and the elaborate *pinnekjøtt*, lamb ribs that have been salted and dried (or salted, smoked, and dried) before being slowly steamed in water over birch twigs, whose aroma infuses the meat. Special seasonal beers are brewed with extra malt and spices. Rice pudding (*risengrynsgrøt*) cold and hot is enjoyed. Another traditional Christmas dessert is *multekrem*, slightly sweetened cloudberries stirred with whipped cream, a mixture often used to fill the intricately patterned, cone-shaped wafers known as *krumkake*. In the past, farm families would set a bowl of rice pudding outside to appease the mischievous barn gnomes at this dark, cold time of year.

When summer arrives, Norwegians head to their *hytter*, rustic cabins where they can return to the simple life and feel like essential Norwegians, if only for a weekend or a few weeks at a time. The days don't just seem endless, they are, especially in the north, where the sun hovers above the horizon all night long. Being at the *hytte* also offers a taste of paradise. When we visited our friends Helge and Berit at their cabin near Brønnøysund, we lived simply but grandly, savoring roasted alpine lamb, panfried lake trout, and extraordinary grilled salmon. Helge rubs salmon fillets with equal amounts

of sugar and salt and leaves them to cure for just ninety minutes before rinsing them. He then places them skin side down on foil on a grill, surrounded by juniper branches, and cooks them, covered, for 10 minutes. Helge's sauce is divine: onions sweated in beer till they caramelize, with a handful of bluish-black crowberries thrown in, along with ground juniper berries and a few sliced young birch leaves. He finishes the sauce with a touch of brown sugar and vinegar.

One afternoon Helge and Berit took us to climb Torghatten, a dramatic granite mountain with a large natural tunnel right through its middle, carved out during the Ice Age—though locals like to say it formed when a troll king threw up his hat to stop an arrow from piercing a maiden trying to escape an evil troll's unwanted advances. The hat turned into Torghatten and the evil troll's arrow traveled right through the mountain to create the dramatic hole. Next we visited Hildurs Urterarium (Hildur's Herbarium), a restaurant and garden where Atle and Laila Tilrem coax more than two hundred plants from the sandy soil. Their bog myrtle flavors schnapps, their lovage goes into salads. The herbarium includes a biblical garden, where we were startled to see Atle's octogenarian father, Thorbjørn, rise up, his towering posture, luxuriant beard, and long, staff-like shovel making him look like Gandalf from *The Lord of the Rings*.

Beyond the gardens Atle and his father have reconstructed a Stone Age dwelling, with enormous doors made from the jaws of sperm whales. A fire pit dominates the circular interior, with carved wooden benches all around. Atle believes in the power of fire. He explained how he likes to "break the ice" among diners, to create a convivial mood. Guests are brought to the hut for aperitifs and seated in a circle around the fire, below the line of smoke that hovers in the air. Then, he claims, magic ensues. Differences dissolve in the fire's uniform glow, and within minutes strangers are sharing stories, regardless of their age, class, shyness, or national origin.

Even without a fire burning, I could sense in that hut the ancient power of the Norwegian coast, the rhythms of its seasons and its tides. But one thing was missing from my experience of Norway. Though I'd been up and down the coast from Stavanger to Kirkenes, I'd never fully explored the country's mountainous interior. So, with my husband as intrepid driver, we set out to encounter isolation. Along the Arctic Circle, in the mountains that border Sweden, the landscape is empty save for deep-green pine trees, dazzlingly blue lakes, and granite outcroppings where spirits surely still lurk. Every so often we spied an opening to the sky, where cows or sheep grazed on alpine pastures. Driving GPS-less, we took one wrong turn after another on precarious roads not intended for low-slung rental sedans, but we consoled ourselves with the beauty of the place and the knowledge that we didn't have to worry about reaching our destination before nightfall, since nightfall wouldn't come for a couple of weeks. Somehow we arrived on time at Sæterstad Gård, an organic farm nestled in the mountains near Hattfjelldal, where Siri Kobberrød and her family raise goats and make fifteen different types of goat cheese. They also farm arctic char, which they served us that evening with chive butter and bearwort, whose leaves, like those of its cousin lovage, have a haunting, celery-like flavor. Bearwort is sometimes used instead of dill for flavoring gravlax in Norway. In her classic *A Modern Herbal* (1931), English herbalist Maud

Grieve writes that "baldmoney" is another name for this plant, linking it through folk etymology to Balder, the Norse god of goodness, perhaps because abundant bearwort is said to indicate good pastureland.

Sæterstad Gård—including our bedroom upstairs—was suffused with the sweet smell of *geitost* from the dairy below. We sampled several varieties, including Siri's version of coffee cheese, here made from goat's milk. Known in Finland as squeaky cheese for the sound it makes when chewed, it is enjoyed with coffee across the whole broad swath of the North. Siri placed four slices of cheese in the bottom of each of our coffee cups, then poured in strong coffee. After drinking down to the dregs, we ate the coffee-infused cheese, enjoying the squeak between our teeth.

When it was time to leave the farm, we said reluctant good-byes and stowed our bags in the car, then turned back to the farm with its wild herbs and domestic animals, an outpost of settlement at the edge of untamed forest and vacant land. We were thinking about Norway's trajectory from poverty to the sudden wealth that enables this remote farmstead to thrive in a way that wouldn't have been possible even fifty years ago. We were wondering where the nearest neighbors were, and whether the deeply Norwegian tradition of *dugnader*—gatherings where people come together to help each other out and share good food and drink—was important to life on the farm.

Just as we were about to drive off, Siri came running out, gesturing for us to come back in. We had neglected to sign the guest book! Siri's request was quite urgent, reminding us that hosting, having guests, remains a privilege to the Norwegians, one that they cherish as they greet each visitor with warmth and the compelling flavors of their land.

VEGETABLES

The entreaty to "Eat your vegetables!" is such a cliché of American childhood that an entire industry revolves around ways to make vegetables attractive to kids. Such thinking is foreign to the Nordic lands, where vegetables are so natural in the diet that they're not really seen as a distinct food category—many Scandinavian cookbooks don't even include a separate chapter on them. You find vegetables in piquant appetizers like Beet Tartare (see page 19), and in mellow main courses like Meatball and Celery Root Stew (see page 175). They sing with fresh flavor and crispness when tossed with vinegar and herbs, as in Swished Cucumbers (see page 102) and Chopped Winter Salad (see page 105). And the whole reason for Finnish Summer Soup is to celebrate the season's first tiny vegetables.

Although you'll find vegetable recipes throughout the book, this chapter highlights a few dishes that make excellent sides. Most involve roots and tubers. Until fairly recently, when produce began flying wantonly across the globe, the Nordic diet was largely restricted to vegetables that could thrive in a harsh climate. While the relatively mild climate of southern Sweden and Denmark allows for greater variety, the North is disadvantaged. The temperatures are colder, and the soil turns progressively poorer. So, most Scandinavians learned to rely on rutabagas, beets, turnips, parsnips, and eventually potatoes, as well as cruciferous crops like cabbage and cauliflower. Besides being rich in nutrients, all of these vegetables are good storage crops, able to last through a long winter. Beets and cabbage especially lend themselves to pickling and brining. And people today still avidly forage for mushrooms and nettles, spruce tips and juniper berries, all of which provide additional vitamins.

I happen to be a huge fan of root vegetables, their crunch when raw and their savory sweetness when slow cooked. But since we all tend to fall into ruts with roots, here are some Scandinavian flavor sensations. All of these recipes will give you an elemental taste of the North.

JERUSALEM ARTICHOKES, OFTEN sold in the States as "sunchokes," are a favorite vegetable in Denmark. I love them for their nutty flavor and creamy texture when baked. Usually I garnish Nordic dishes with bright green herbs like parsley or dill, but here I let the unabashedly brown tubers and mushrooms speak for themselves, since they're such elemental gifts from the earth.

Bagte jordskokker med svampe

 # BAKED JERUSALEM ARTICHOKES
AND MUSHROOMS

SERVES 4 TO 6

1 pound Jerusalem artichokes, scrubbed and cut into ½-inch slices

½ cup crème fraîche

½ teaspoon salt

Freshly ground pepper

3 sprigs thyme

8 ounces wild mushrooms, coarsely chopped

1 tablespoon butter, melted

Preheat the oven to 375°F. Lightly butter a shallow baking dish just large enough to hold the Jerusalem artichokes in a single layer.

In a bowl, toss the Jerusalem artichokes with the crème fraîche and ¼ teaspoon of the salt. Season with pepper. Turn into the baking dish and tuck in the thyme sprigs. Cover with aluminum foil and bake 30 minutes.

Meanwhile, in another bowl, toss the mushrooms with the melted butter and the remaining ¼ teaspoon of salt. Season with pepper. Remove the artichokes from the oven, stir in the mushrooms, and continue baking, uncovered, until the artichokes are tender and beautifully browned, about 15 minutes more. Serve hot or warm.

CAMILLA PLUM IS the mother of Denmark's ecological food movement, having opened the country's first organic restaurant in 1992. With my friend Eja I was lucky enough to visit Camilla's inspiring organic farm, Fuglebjerggaard, about an hour north of Copenhagen, where she grows more than 200 types of vegetables, saves heirloom seeds, and bottles all sorts of sauces and preserves.

The recipe below was inspired by Camilla's cookbook *The Scandinavian Kitchen*, where she calls for mixing root vegetables with elderflower cordial. Because this cordial isn't easy to find in the States, I've substituted St-Germain elderflower liqueur, an admittedly extravagant choice but a lovely one. This is a beautiful autumn or winter side dish, nicely balanced between sweet onions and apples and tart lemon and vinegar.

Ovnbagte æbler med løg, citron og hyld

 # ROASTED APPLES AND ONIONS
WITH LEMON AND ELDERFLOWER
SERVES 4 TO 6

1¾ pounds yellow onions (about 4)

1¾ pounds tart apples, such as Winesap (about 4)

1 teaspoon salt

½ teaspoon freshly ground pepper

¼ teaspoon fresh thyme

Grated zest of 1 lemon

4 tablespoons butter, melted

¼ cup St-Germain elderflower liqueur

1 tablespoon cider vinegar

1 tablespoon freshly squeezed lemon juice

Preheat the oven to 425°F. Peel the onions and peel and core the apples. Cut each onion and apple into 16 wedges and place in a large, shallow roasting pan. Season with the salt, pepper, thyme, and lemon zest, then pour the melted butter over the onions and apples and toss them to coat evenly.

In a bowl, stir together the liqueur, vinegar, and lemon juice. Pour over the onions and apples and toss once again.

Roast the onions and apples, stirring occasionally, until they are very caramelized, about 1¼ hours.

THE FIRST TIME I saw the name of this dish in Swedish, I immediately thought of swamps and bogs, not the best association for something I was about to eat. While it's true that Swedish *svamp* and English "swamp" share an etymology, please don't let linguistics deter you from making this toast. It's Swedish comfort food at its best, quickly prepared and utterly satisfying. And don't worry if you can't find chanterelles. Any wild mushrooms will do.

Svamptoast

 **MUSHROOM TOAST**

SERVES 4

8 ounces chanterelles

3 tablespoons butter

1 tablespoon finely chopped red onion

3 tablespoons heavy cream

1 tablespoon finely chopped parsley

1 teaspoon freshly squeezed lemon juice

¼ teaspoon salt

Freshly ground pepper

4 slices country bread

Pick over the mushrooms and wipe away any forest debris with a damp paper towel. Chop them medium fine. Melt 1 tablespoon of the butter in a frying pan over medium-low heat and add the mushrooms and onion. Sauté until the moisture released by the mushrooms evaporates, about 5 minutes. Stir in the cream and parsley and heat gently to thicken. Stir in the salt, lemon juice, and season with pepper.

While the mushrooms are cooking, in a frying pan over medium heat panfry the bread in the remaining 2 tablespoons of butter until golden on both sides, about 4 minutes.

Spoon the mushroom mixture evenly onto the toast slices and serve immediately.

I FIRST ENCOUNTERED butter-steamed potatoes as a newlywed living in Stockholm. I had carried *James Beard's Delights and Prejudices* across the ocean to serve as my kitchen bible. There I discovered a recipe for *pommes fondantes*, tiny, peeled potatoes steamed in nothing but butter over low heat. That year in Sweden I spent a lot of time standing over the stove, shaking the pot to make sure the potatoes didn't burn. Now, though, I make these darlings in a much more carefree manner, one I discovered in Norway. For all their ease, they are just as delectable.

Smørdampete nypoteter

BUTTER-STEAMED NEW POTATOES

SERVES 4

1 pound tiny new potatoes, no larger than 1 inch in diameter (about 2 dozen), unpeeled

4 tablespoons butter

½ teaspoon salt

3 tablespoons finely chopped fresh dill

Preheat the oven to 300°F. Scrub the potatoes and drain them in a colander.

Place the butter in a small gratin dish just large enough to hold the potatoes. Set the dish in the oven for the butter to melt, then add the potatoes and salt, and toss with the butter. Cover the dish tightly with foil and bake until the potatoes are tender, about 1 hour.

Sprinkle the potatoes with the dill and serve immediately, right from the gratin dish.

THE GORGEOUS CARAMEL coating on these potatoes belies their simplicity—all you need are potatoes, sugar, butter, and a steady wrist for shaking the pan as the potatoes glaze. My friend Bodil Wilson taught me how to perfect them: use waxy potatoes, and don't let your attention wander as the potatoes cook or the caramel will turn hard "and bitter. These potatoes taste wonderful with roast pork, meatballs, or sausage, and are a must on the Danish Christmas table with roast duck or goose.

Brunede kartofler

 # CARAMELIZED POTATOES

SERVES 4

1 pound small boiling potatoes (each about 2 inches wide)

¼ cup sugar

3 tablespoons salted butter

Boil the potatoes in a large pot of salted water until tender, about 15 minutes. Drain, and peel them when they are cool enough to handle. The potatoes can be made ahead of time and set aside.

Melt the sugar over medium heat in a small cast-iron frying pan just large enough to hold the potatoes in a single layer. Don't stir while the sugar is melting; just shake the pan back and forth to assist the melting process. When the sugar has melted and is just beginning to take on color, add the butter and allow it to sizzle and froth with the sugar for a minute. If the mixture seems too thick, add a little water to make it more sauce-like so that the potatoes will glaze evenly. Then add the potatoes, holding a pot lid as a shield to prevent the hot caramel from spattering onto you.

Lower the heat to medium-low. Shake the pan and toss the potatoes until they are evenly glazed, 15 to 20 minutes. Using a rubber spatula to turn the potatoes helps glaze them more evenly. Be sure not to cover the pan, or the glaze will lose its shine. Serve immediately.

NOTE: If you're not serving the potatoes right away, you can reheat them by adding a little water to the pan and tossing the potatoes until the glaze has melted again.

NO ONE'S SURE who Jansson was, but once you taste this dish you'll know why he was so tempted. Rich with cream and a touch of sweetness, Jansson's Temptation is admittedly indulgent fare. No wonder its popularity has crossed borders!

For this dish to succeed, you'll need to buy Swedish anchovies (*Sprattus sprattus*), which are not the salty fish we often associate with Italian cuisine (see Sources). They are delicate sprats that have been cured with sugar, salt, and spices like cinnamon and sandalwood; they virtually melt into the potatoes as they bake. Think of this dish as a Nordic version of scalloped potatoes, with a surprise inside.

Janssons frestelse

 **JANSSON'S TEMPTATION**

SERVES 4

2 medium yellow onions

3 tablespoons butter

2 pounds large waxy potatoes, such as red potatoes (about 4)

1 (4.4-ounce) can Swedish anchovies

Freshly ground pepper

1 cup heavy cream

Halve the onions lengthwise, then cut them into ¼-inch slices.

Melt the butter in a large skillet over medium-low heat, add the onions, and sauté until soft but not brown, about 10 minutes.

Preheat the oven to 400°F. Fill a large bowl with ice water. Peel the potatoes and cut them lengthwise into ¼-inch strips.

Butter a 1½-quart gratin dish. Spread half of the potatoes on the bottom of the dish. Top them with the onions and then the anchovies, reserving the anchovy brine from the can. Grind a generous amount of pepper on top. Cover with the remaining potatoes. Drizzle the potatoes with the anchovy brine from the can, then pour the cream evenly over the top.

Bake until the potatoes are tender and the top is crusty and brown, 50 to 60 minutes.

THE DANES ARE enormously fond of red cabbage. In the summer it adds crunch to salads and open-faced sandwiches. In the winter it's braised until soft, a perfect companion to all sorts of meat, from meatballs to roast pork, duck, and goose. Its red-letter day is Christmas, when it's part of the trinity of roast fowl, caramelized potatoes, and red cabbage. Its bracing flavor cuts the meat's richness and brings color to an otherwise brown palette.

This recipe comes from Bodil Wilson, a superb home cook who still likes to make Danish specialties even though she has lived in the States for more than fifty years. Trained as a teacher of home economics, Bodil enjoys varying her cabbage recipe, sometimes adding apples, other times caraway seed, as is common in the southern part of Jutland. If you like your cabbage sweet, you can substitute the Danish liqueurs Cherry Heering or Cherry Kijafa for half a cup of the tart currant juice. When Bodil makes sweet and sour red cabbage for Christmas, she often stirs in an 8-ounce can of drained mandarin oranges just before serving, for a bright and fruity finish.

Rødkål

SWEET-AND-SOUR RED CABBAGE

SERVES 6

6 dried apricots

6 dried peaches

6 dried pears

Boiling water, for soaking

2 pounds red cabbage

4 tablespoons butter

3 tablespoons red wine vinegar

1 tablespoon rice vinegar

2 tablespoons sugar

1 cup unsweetened red or black currant juice

6 tablespoons red currant jelly (or a little more, to taste)

1 teaspoon salt

Freshly ground pepper

The day before serving, place the apricots, peaches, and pears in a small bowl and pour in enough boiling water to cover them. Let the fruit and water cool, then cover with plastic wrap and refrigerate for 24 hours.

The next day, drain the fruit and cut it into ¼-inch pieces. With a box grater or food processor, shred the cabbage medium fine. Melt the butter in a large skillet over medium heat, add the cabbage and fruit, and turn to coat with butter. Stir in the vinegars, sugar, and currant juice. Cover the pan, lower the heat, and simmer until the cabbage is just tender, about 30 minutes.

Stir in the jelly and salt, and season with pepper. Continue to cook for a few minutes, until the jelly melts. The cabbage can be prepared several days ahead of time and kept chilled. Reheat in a skillet before serving.

UNTIL I FINALLY tasted the vegetable, my only association with the word "rutabaga" came from a children's book, Carl Sandburg's *Rootabaga Stories*, so I always thought it was some kind of nonsensical vegetable. But for many immigrants to America, the rutabaga represented something else, something distinctly not whimsical—poverty food, which they ate boiled and unadorned and all the time. So reliant were Scandinavians on this vitamin-rich root that it came to be known in English as a "swede," a metonym for the hungry people who had to consume it.

Still, I hope you'll take another look (and taste!). Rutabaga, especially in this Finnish Christmas pudding, has a wonderfully mellow flavor and a beautiful golden color—a nice change from mashed potatoes. Because I like the pudding with a bit of texture, I mash the rutabaga by hand, but if you prefer a smooth puree, you can use a food processor. I also like to use rye or whole wheat bread crumbs in the topping for more depth of flavor, but any bread you have on hand will be fine.

Lanttulaattiko

 # RUTABAGA PUDDING

SERVES 6 TO 8

2 pounds rutabaga (1 medium), peeled and cut into 1½-inch cubes

2 eggs

½ cup heavy cream or milk

½ teaspoon salt

½ teaspoon freshly grated nutmeg

Dash of ground allspice

¼ cup fine dried bread crumbs

2 tablespoons butter, melted, plus 1 tablespoon butter, cut into small pieces

2 tablespoons fresh bread crumbs

Preheat the oven to 350°F. Butter a 1½-quart soufflé dish.

Boil the rutabaga in a large pot of salted water to cover until tender, around 30 minutes. Drain, then transfer the pieces to a large bowl and mash.

Beat in the eggs one at a time, then stir in the cream, salt, nutmeg, allspice, dried bread crumbs, and melted butter. Turn the mixture into the prepared dish.

Run a fork a few times across the surface of the puree to make a wavy pattern. Finely crumble the fresh bread crumbs and sprinkle them into the grooves, then dot the pudding with the small pieces of butter.

Bake, uncovered, until the pudding is puffed and golden, about 1 hour. Serve hot.

RATHER THAN SUCCUMB to the doldrums of winter, I try to be Nordic and embrace the bitter cold and the dark. And that sometimes means playing with fire! We have a wood-fired oven in our kitchen, where we bake bread and pizza and like to roast meat and vegetables near the coals. Recently we began looking for culinary ways to use some of the ash, and this New Nordic technique for coating root vegetables has become a favorite. When you smear celery root with a paste of salt and ash, the interior turns out wonderfully creamy and perfectly seasoned. Lacking a wood-fired oven, you can use ash from a regular fireplace or from a grill, as long as it comes from hardwood.

Salt- og askebagt selleri
SALT- AND ASH-BAKED CELERY ROOT

SERVES 4

1 small celery root (about 14 ounces)

2½ cups salt

½ cup fireplace ash

½ cup water, or as needed

2 tablespoons butter

2 tablespoons chopped fresh parsley

Preheat the oven to 350°F. Scrub the celery root. In a small bowl, stir together the salt, ash, and water to make a paste that holds together when you squeeze it with your hand (the amount of water will depend on how dense the ash is).

Spread the paste all over the celery root, pressing down so that it adheres, and place the celery root in an ovenproof dish. Bake until you can easily insert a small knife, about 2 hours.

Just before the celery root comes out of the oven, melt the butter in a small pan over low heat, then stir in the parsley. Set aside.

Remove the celery root from the oven and crack the crust open with a meat mallet. With a small paring knife, peel the charred celery root, then slice it lengthwise and arrange on a platter. Drizzle the parsleyed butter over the top and serve immediately.

THIS VIVID GREEN puree captures the essence of spring. I enjoyed it in mid-May at my dear friend Scott Givot's cabin (or *hytte*) on Heggholmen, an island in the Oslo fjord. Scott and I walked down to a dock in Oslo, where Scott's partner, Lars Røtterud, met us in his motorboat. The first peas had just begun to appear in the markets, so Lars whipped up this puree to accompany the salt-roasted turbot he'd made for dinner. Sweet and fresh tasting, it doesn't even need seasoning.

Because I can't reliably find sweet fresh peas where I live, I tested the recipe both ways, with fresh peas and frozen ones. A 9-ounce package of frozen peas yields just the right amount.

Erter og aspargespuré

PEA AND ASPARAGUS PUREE

SERVES 3 OR 4

1½ cups fresh or frozen peas

2 tablespoons butter

4 ounces asparagus, trimmed and cut into ½-inch lengths

¼ cup water

If you're using frozen peas, thaw them and drain them well in a colander.

Melt the butter in a medium skillet over medium-low heat, then stir in the asparagus and sauté until slightly softened but not brown, about 3 minutes. Add the peas and water and cover the pan. Steam until soft, about 3 minutes more.

Transfer the vegetables to the bowl of a food processor and pulse until pureed. Don't make it too smooth—it should remain textured. Serve right away or at room temperature.

I LIKE TO think of these tasty vegetable cakes as Nordic latkes. They're wonderfully creamy inside yet have a crisp finish, thanks to the grated vegetables. This recipe, adapted from a small cookbook published by Savonia University of Applied Sciences, lends itself to experimentation. Using mashed potatoes as the base, you can try different proportions of the grated vegetables, depending on your preferences, or add others you like, such as turnips or leeks.

Kasvispihvit

 # ROOT VEGETABLE CAKES

SERVES 4 AS A MAIN COURSE OR 8 AS A SIDE DISH

2 boiling potatoes (about 1 pound)

2 large carrots (about 8 ounces)

6 ounces celery root

1 large parsnip (about 4 ounces)

1 yellow onion, finely chopped

2 eggs, lightly beaten

½ cup finely chopped fresh herbs (such as chervil, dill, parsley, and thyme)

1 teaspoon salt

Freshly ground pepper

Canola oil, for frying

Boil the potatoes in a large pot of salted water until tender, about 20 minutes. Drain, and when cool enough to handle, peel them, then transfer them to a large bowl and mash.

While the potatoes are boiling, peel and grate the carrots, celery root, and parsnip with the grating disk of a food processor. Stir all of the grated vegetables along with the chopped onion into the mashed potatoes. Then add the eggs, herbs, salt, and pepper to taste, mixing well until a solid mass forms. I find it best to work the mass with my hands.

In a large, deep skillet, pour the oil to a depth of ¼ inch. The oil is hot enough when a droplet of water tossed onto it sizzles.

Shape the vegetable mixture into 3-inch patties and slide them into the hot oil. Cook over medium heat until browned, about 8 minutes. Then flip the cakes and cook the other side until golden, about 8 minutes more. Drain on paper towels and transfer to a serving platter. Serve hot.

THESE STRIKING PANCAKES are a Finnish favorite. Unlike fluffy American-style pancakes, they are much thinner and more crepe-like (the word *ohukkaat* means "the thin ones"), and they have a moist interior. Traditional spinach pancakes are baked on a *muurikka*, a large, slightly concave cast-iron griddle designed for cooking outdoors over an open fire. When made in this special pan, the pancakes are large, with lacy edges. But how many of us have a *muurikka*? Although a southwestern *discada*—a plow-disk "wok"—would be a fine substitute, the recipe here is adapted for indoor use on a *plättlagg* (a Swedish pancake pan) or any other griddle or cast-iron skillet. Maria Planting has told me about the wonderful spinach pancakes of her childhood, served with lingonberry preserves. I think they make an excellent platform for appetizers when topped with whitefish roe and a dab of sour cream.

Pinaatti-ohukkaat

SPINACH PANCAKES

SERVES 4 TO 6

5 ounces frozen spinach (about 2 cups chopped), thawed and squeezed dry

2 eggs

2 cups whole milk

1 cup flour

½ teaspoon salt

A few grindings of white pepper

Pinch of freshly grated nutmeg

Butter, for cooking

Place the spinach in a blender with the eggs and whir until the spinach is finely chopped. Add milk, flour, salt, pepper, and nutmeg and puree until bubbly, about 30 seconds. The batter will be thin, as for crepes. Let the batter stand for at least 10 minutes before using. The batter can be made well ahead of time and refrigerated for up to 2 days. (I leave it in the blender jar so that if the batter separates, I can easily whir it for a few seconds to reblend.)

Place a generous dab of butter in each indentation of a *plättlagg*, or in a cast-iron skillet, and set over medium-low heat. When the pan is hot, pour a scant tablespoon of the batter into each indentation, or directly onto the skillet. Be careful not to use too much batter or the pancakes won't cook through. Cook until tiny bubbles appear on the surface of each pancake, about 3 minutes, then carefully flip them with a small, blunt knife and cook for about 3 minutes more, until the edges are crisp and the pancakes are lightly browned and cooked through.

The pancakes can be served right away, but if you want to use them for appetizers they can be set aside at room temperature for a couple of hours.

DESSERTS

Visitors to Scandinavia are often amazed to find so many tempting bakeries, pastry shops, and candy stores. The regional sweet tooth is also evident in Sweden's *lördagsgodis*, "Saturday candy," which leads to sweetfests each weekend. This ritual dates back to the 1930s, when the government sought to control tooth decay by encouraging people to limit their candy consumption to just once a week.

Honey was the original sweetener, used in gingersnaps and spice cakes throughout the North. True Nordic desserts consist of the sweet things found in nature, the seasonal berries and fruits. They are eaten plain or pressed for their juice, which is made into soups or starch-thickened puddings. Many of today's best-loved desserts arose from frugality, like the apple puddings made from poached apples layered with toasted bread crumbs and cream. Leftover bits of dough were fried into crisp treats, which eventually morphed into today's intricate rosettes made from a liquid batter.

When sugar and fine wheat flour became more affordable, just over a century ago, baking came into its own. Women in rural areas, especially in Finland and Sweden, gathered for "coffee tables" to show off their baking skills and to socialize. Up to twenty different baked goods appeared on these tables, from cookies to plain cakes to sweet breads and layer cakes, all served with strong coffee. Meanwhile, in urban settings, the late nineteenth century saw the rise of a gilded coffee shop culture, in which the beau monde lingered over coffee and European-style pastries in elegant settings. Denmark's pastry chefs so excelled at making the *viennoiserie* they had learned from Viennese masters that Americans still think of these pastries as Danish.

The Nordic countries share a love for almonds, cardamom, cinnamon, and vanilla, which find their way into a multitude of desserts. Not surprisingly, sweet offerings change with the seasons, as the warm spices of winter—ginger and cloves, allspice and cinnamon—give way to summer's prized flavors of berries and orchard fruits.

THIS CAKE IS, quite simply, a showstopper. With mounds of fresh strawberries layered between billows of whipped cream and disks of slightly chewy almond meringue, it tastes as fabulous as it looks.

Mansikkakakku

 ## STRAWBERRY MERINGUE CAKE

SERVES 8

1 cup blanched almonds

1½ cups plus 2 tablespoons sugar

6 egg whites

Pinch of salt

1½ cups heavy cream

¼ teaspoon pure vanilla extract

2 cups strawberries, sliced

Preheat oven to 350°F. Place the almonds on a baking sheet and toast until just golden, 6 to 8 minutes. Lower heat to 250°F.

Transfer the almonds to the bowl of a food processor. Add ½ cup of the sugar and pulse until the almonds are finely ground.

Place the egg whites in the bowl of a stand mixer and beat on high speed until foamy. Add the salt and gradually beat in 1 cup of the sugar until stiff peaks form. Continue beating on the highest speed until you have a stiff, shiny meringue, about 3 minutes more. Gently fold in the almond mixture.

Line a large baking sheet with parchment paper. With a spatula, carefully spread the meringue into two 8-inch rounds, smoothing the tops. Bake until pale gold, about 1 hour. Then turn off the heat and prop the oven door ajar with the handle of a wooden spoon. Let the meringues dry in the oven for 2 hours more, until no longer sticky to the touch.

When the meringue layers are ready, whip the cream with the remaining 2 tablespoons of sugar and the vanilla until stiff but not dry. Carefully transfer one meringue layer to a cake plate. Spread ½ cup of the whipped cream over the layer and top the cream with half of the strawberries. Cover the strawberries with another ½ cup of the whipped cream. Place the second meringue layer on top of the filling. Decoratively pipe the remaining ½ cup of whipped cream around the edge of the meringue layer, and fill the center with the remaining sliced strawberries.

Refrigerate the cake for 1 hour before serving to allow the flavors to meld. It can be held for up to 4 hours before it begins to weep. Let it stand at room temperature for 15 minutes before serving.

THIS BEAUTIFUL SUMMER recipe comes from my dear friend Stefanie Jandl. As an art historian, she has an eye for color, and this pudding simply vibrates with red. It also has emotional resonance for her. As soon as the summer berries ripened in the Danish countryside, traditional *rødgrød* would appear on the menu at Asminderød Kro, the country inn and restaurant her grandmother owned in Fredensborg. After drizzling fresh cream onto the pudding, Stefanie's grandmother (*mormor*) would reverently point out the likeness to the red-and-white Danish flag.

Mormor always put the cooked berries through a strainer, but Stefanie's mother, who lived in California, modernized the recipe in the late 1970s when she got her first food processor, pureeing the berries to retain all their nutrients and fiber. Stefanie's own iteration was to use an immersion blender, but in retesting the recipe for this book, she once again tried her grandmother's style and declared it the best. I have to agree! While the food-processed and blended versions yield delicious, full-bodied *rødgrød*, they don't have the intense berry flavor, silky texture, and luminous red color of the pudding presented here. If you're lucky enough to find fresh red currants, which are traditional in Denmark, by all means add them to the mix.

Rødgrød

RED BERRY PUDDING

SERVES 4 TO 6

2 pounds ripe, fresh strawberries and raspberries

¼ cup plus ⅓ cup cold water

¼ cup sugar, plus more for serving

3 tablespoons cornstarch or arrowroot

Light cream, for serving

Hull the strawberries and cut them in half or in quarters if they are large. Place the berries in a 4-quart saucepan along with ¼ cup of the water and ¼ cup of the sugar. Bring the berry mixture to a boil, then lower the heat and cook at a gentle boil, stirring occasionally, until the berries are mostly liquid, 5 to 7 minutes. With a fine-mesh strainer, strain the liquid into a 2-quart saucepan, discarding the pulp.

Dissolve the cornstarch in ⅓ cup of cold water. Bring the strained liquid to a gentle boil and add the dissolved cornstarch, stirring constantly until the mixture thickens, about 1 minute. Remove from the heat and pour into a large serving bowl. Refrigerate for at least 2 hours.

To serve, spoon the chilled pudding into individual bowls. Drizzle with light cream and sprinkle with sugar.

FINNISH IS A famously difficult language, and the six months I lived in Finland weren't nearly enough for me to achieve fluency. But I did learn how to survive, by which I mean buy food, order food, and talk about food with my friends. The culinary words tripped off my tongue, and even today I repeat *mustikkapiirakka*–blueberry pie–like a mantra. Maybe it was my mantra. Finnish blueberry pies come in all sorts of styles, from tarts to deep-dish pies to kuchen-like cakes. The rustic version below is a specialty of Savo, a region in eastern Finland on the border with Russia.

Mustikkakukko is like a New England slump or grunt, juicy with berries and rich with buttery dough. Old-time Savo residents call the dish *rättänä*, an untranslatable word, but more recently the name *kukko*, or "rooster," has come to be used. Other similarly shaped foods baked with rye dough carry the same name–*kalakukko* is a fish rooster, *lanttukukko* a rutabaga one. Some creative cook may have thought that a crust generously bulging with filling resembled a strutting rooster's belly. Or *kukko* could be a distortion of *kakko*, the term for "bread" in central Finland. I like the image of a rooster.

What makes this dessert distinctively Finnish and beautifully homespun is the use of rye flour. I recommend King Arthur medium rye for this recipe, but if you only have stone-ground rye, whir it briefly in the food processor to get a finer texture. The dough will be crumbly. Pat the dough out for the bottom of the crust. For the top, just break off pieces of the dough, flatten them slightly, and dot them over the berries.

Mustikkakukko
BLUEBERRY "ROOSTER"

SERVES 8

12 tablespoons (1½ sticks) butter, at room temperature

¼ cup plus 10 tablespoons sugar

1½ cups medium rye flour

½ cup plus 1 tablespoon flour

2 teaspoons baking powder

½ teaspoon salt

5 cups fresh blueberries

Ice cream or whipped cream, for serving (optional)

Cream the butter with ¼ cup of the sugar. In a small bowl, stir together the rye flour, ½ cup of the all-purpose flour, the baking powder, and the salt. Pour the flour mixture into the creamed butter mixture and stir until a very soft dough forms. With your hands, shape the dough into a ball, and then into a flat disk. Cover the dough in plastic wrap and refrigerate for 1 hour.

Meanwhile, in a bowl, stir the blueberries with the remaining 10 tablespoons of sugar and the remaining 1 tablespoon of flour.

Preheat the oven to 400°F. Butter a 10-inch deep-dish pie plate. With floured hands, break off about two-thirds of the dough and press it on the bottom and sides of the dish. Spread the blueberries in the dough-lined pie plate and top them with the remaining dough. Bake until browned, about 35 minutes. Serve with whipped cream or ice cream.

HAVING GROWN UP with Jell-O, I discovered how beautiful gelatin can be only after experimenting in my own kitchen. This jewel-like dessert captures red raspberries in a deep purple suspension. Less gelatin in the mixture means that it takes longer to firm up in the refrigerator, but you can decrease the chilling time by making individual servings in small bowls. Any container will do, but glass adds to the shimmer.

I devised this recipe after tasting jellied strawberries with angelica cream at Tertin Kartano in Mikkeli, Finland. Lacking angelica, I played on the idea of tart fruit in gentle gelatin, the contrast between bright flavors and soft textures. Like many other Finnish berry desserts, these jellied berries are more refreshing than sweet. So I sometimes sprinkle them with a little raw sugar and drizzle with heavy cream just before serving.

Hyytelöityjä vadelmia

JELLIED RASPBERRIES

SERVES 8

½ cup cold water

2 envelopes (2 tablespoons) unflavored gelatin

3½ cups sweetened black currant juice

2 tablespoons sugar

3 cups fresh raspberries

Measure the ½ cup cold water directly into a 2-quart Pyrex measuring cup. Sprinkle the gelatin over the water, then stir to moisten it. Let sit until the gelatin softens, about 3 minutes.

Meanwhile, in a saucepan, bring the black currant juice and sugar just to the boiling point. Slowly pour the juice mixture over the softened gelatin, stirring constantly. Continue to stir for about 2 minutes, until the gelatin is completely dissolved.

Refrigerate the gelatin mixture until it is slightly thickened and syrupy, 2½ to 2¾ hours. When it is the right consistency, pour the mixture to a depth of 1 inch into an 8- or 9-inch glass dish. Gently arrange 1½ cups of the raspberries over the gelatin mixture in a single layer. Refrigerate the gelatin remaining in the Pyrex cup, as well as the gelatin and berries in the glass dish, for 15 minutes, then pour another layer of gelatin over the raspberries to just cover them. Top with the remaining 1½ cups raspberries and pour the rest of the gelatin mixture over them—the raspberries should be visible through the gelatin. Depending on the shape of your dish, you may not use all the berries.

Refrigerate until completely set, about 2 hours more. To store, stretch plastic wrap over the edges of the dish, making sure that it doesn't touch the surface of the gelatin. The dessert will keep for up to 3 days.

ALMOND PASTE IS the essential ingredient, the sine qua non, of Scandinavian baking. It appears in breads, cakes, cookies, tarts—you name it. I'm addicted to Swedish *mazariner*—miniature tartlets of butter-, sugar-, and egg-enriched almond paste baked in a cookie-like crust—but since each one has to be shaped by hand they're time-consuming to make. How happy I was, then, to discover Norway's *kransekakestenger*, marzipan cookies that take no time at all. They're like miniature versions of the famous *kransekake*, that queen of Norwegian (and Danish) cakes, a lavish multistory ring cake constructed of ground almonds, egg whites, and sugar. These small *kransekakestenger* offer the same almondy satisfaction but without all the fuss. A bakery staple, they're packaged on Norwegian Constitution Day with red, white, and blue ribbons to celebrate the colors of the Norwegian flag.

In an ideal world I'd hand-grind the almonds in a nut grinder, which yields the best, fluffy texture, but a food processor works nearly as well, as long as you're careful not to overprocess the nuts. The dough can be made ahead of time and chilled overnight before using.

Kransekakestenger

 **MARZIPAN BARS**

MAKES 2 DOZEN

1 cup blanched almonds

1 cup natural (unblanched) almonds

2¼ cups confectioners' sugar, plus more for dusting

2 egg whites

¼ teaspoon pure almond extract

6 ounces semisweet chocolate

2 to 3 tablespoons heavy cream

Grind the blanched and natural almonds very fine in a food processor, making sure to stop processing before they turn oily. Add the confectioners' sugar and pulse a few times until the mixture is powder.

Transfer the almond powder to a bowl and stir in the egg whites and almond extract until a firm dough forms. Shape the dough into a ball, cover in plastic wrap, and refrigerate for at least 2 hours.

When ready to bake, preheat the oven to 400°F. Line 2 baking sheets with parchment paper. Cut the chilled dough into quarters. Dust your hands with confectioners' sugar and shape each quarter into a log. Cut each log into 6 pieces. Roll each piece into a 3-inch bar between your palms and place the bars 2 inches apart on the baking sheets. Bake until pale gold, about 10 minutes.

While the cookies are cooling, in a heavy-bottomed pan over very low heat, melt the chocolate with the heavy cream. Depending on the chocolate, you may need to add a little more cream to give it a dipping consistency.

Release the cooled cookies from the parchment paper with a spatula. Dip about ½ inch of each end into the chocolate and set the cookies on racks to dry. If the chocolate hardens before you've finished dipping all of the cookies, just reheat it gently.

THESE SMALL, RASPBERRY-FILLED cakes are conceptually similar to American thumb-print cookies, but far more buttery and delectable. This recipe comes from Helsinki chef Nick Victorzon. The cakes take only minutes to prepare—and even less time to disappear!

Hallongrottor

 # RASPBERRY GROTTOES

MAKES 20 SMALL CAKES

1 cup butter, at room temperature

1 cup sugar

¼ teaspoon pure vanilla extract or 1 tablespoon vanilla sugar

2¼ cups flour

1½ teaspoons baking powder

¼ cup thick raspberry jam

Preheat the oven to 350°F. Cream the butter with the sugar. Stir in the vanilla.

In a small bowl, stir together the flour and baking powder. Pour the flour mixture into the creamed butter mixture and stir until a stiff, dry dough forms. With your hands, gently knead the dough until smooth, adding a few drops of heavy cream, if necessary.

Line twenty 2-inch paper muffin cups on a baking sheet. Divide the dough into 20 pieces by first cutting into quarters, and then shaping 5 balls from each quarter. Place each ball in a muffin cup. With your thumb, make an indentation on the top of each ball, pinching any cracked edges together. Fill with about ½ teaspoon of jam. Bake until just golden, about 18 minutes. Let the cakes cool on the baking sheet for 5 minutes, then transfer to a rack to finish cooling.

THE STORY BEHIND this now-classic Finnish and Swedish confection gives us a glimpse into history. Karl Fazer, the founder of Finland's great confectionery empire, discovered the Russian fudge called *tyanushki* in 1866 when he moved to Saint Petersburg to apprentice at a famous pastry shop there. He brought the recipe back to Helsinki, where he opened his own pastry shop in 1891, and adapted it for use as a filling and topping for what became the company's signature cake, which is still sold today.

So imagine my joy and surprise when I learned that Maria Planting, my host, great friend, and guide to all things culinary in Finland, is the great-granddaughter of Karl Fazer! It was Maria who introduced me to yet another version of this beautiful medley of cream, sugar, and vanilla, a luscious sauce that she served over fresh raspberries as we contemplated the rocky shores of the Finnish archipelago. My swoons of pleasure caused her to run inside to retrieve some frozen cranberries to give me a thrilling sense of *tjinuski* in winter, when the hot caramel hardens on hitting the still-frozen berries. Later, in Finland's far north, we tasted *tjinuski* simmered in a skillet over an open fire, then poured over "squeaky cheese" and topped with cloudberry jam—an improbable but delicious trio of flavors. *Tjinuski* is perhaps most traditional when served for dessert at an August crayfish party, but it's a delight at any time of year. It keeps forever in the refrigerator and needs only gentle heating to return to a pourable consistency.

Because this sauce is basically just sweetened cream, the flavor of the cream is all-important. Ultra-pasteurized doesn't taste as good, which is why I recommend against it, though it would work fine in the recipe.

Tjinuski

CARAMEL CREAM

MAKES ABOUT 1 PINT

2 cups sugar

2 cups heavy cream (not ultra-pasteurized)

1 vanilla bean

4 cups fresh raspberries or frozen cranberries

Place the sugar and cream in a 4-quart heavy-bottomed saucepan. With a small, sharp knife, slit the vanilla bean lengthwise and scrape the seeds into the cream. Bring to a boil, stirring to dissolve the sugar, then lower the heat and cook at a low boil for about 1 hour. The mixture will bubble and foam as it cooks, especially on stirring. When the mixture turns a rich caramel color and thickens slightly, it is ready.

Cool slightly and drizzle the cream over fresh raspberries; in the winter, serve hot over frozen cranberries.

Store any leftovers at cool room temperature for up to a couple of days, or refrigerate.

I ADAPTED THIS recipe from one given me by Trine Hahnemann, Danish cookbook writer extraordinaire. Trine made me a gorgeous lunch at her Copenhagen home—panfried plaice dusted with rye meal, fresh cod roe with lemon mayonnaise, roast pork with pickled beet and kale salad. Dessert was charming "potato" cakes, which aren't potato at all but custard-filled choux pastries draped with marzipan and dusted with cocoa to resemble the potatoes that Danes so love.

Finding good almond paste for the marzipan is a challenge here in the States. Trine uses a paste with 60 percent almonds, but even our widely available imported Danish almond paste contains only 45 percent almonds, with sugar making up the rest. Some marketing gurus must have decided that Americans just want sweet. Worse yet is the similarly packaged "marzipan" on grocery store shelves, which contains even less almond and is even more cloyingly sweet. Sigh. For desserts like this, where the almond component is crucial, I splurge on excellent California almond paste that contains 66 percent almonds (see Sources).

These playful "potato" cakes are a good choice for entertaining, since the various parts can be prepared ahead of time and assembled just before serving.

Kartoffelkager

"POTATO" CAKES

SERVES 8

PASTRY

¾ cup flour

Pinch of salt

¾ cup water

5 tablespoons butter

4 eggs, at room temperature

FILLING

1½ cups whole milk

1 vanilla bean

¼ cup sugar

¼ cup cornstarch

Pinch of salt

3 egg yolks

¼ cup heavy cream

To make the pastry, measure out the flour and salt into a bowl and have ready next to the stove. In a saucepan, heat the water and butter over medium. When the water-butter mixture comes to a boil, remove the pan from the heat, and with a wooden spoon, quickly stir in the flour and salt mixture all at once to make a firm, smooth paste, stirring vigorously. Return the pan to low heat and continue to stir the mixture vigorously for another minute or two, until it pulls away from the sides of the pan. Remove the pan from the heat. Make an indentation in the center of the dough and, working quickly, crack an egg into it, stirring rapidly until the egg is incorporated into the dough. Repeat with the remaining 3 eggs, adding them one at a time and stirring well after each addition. Continue to stir vigorously for another minute or so until the mixture is smooth and soft peaks form.

Confectioners' sugar, for sprinkling

8 ounces almond paste

1 tablespoon unsweetened cocoa powder

Preheat the oven 425°F. Place a piece of parchment paper on a baking sheet. Transfer the dough to a pastry bag with a plain ¾-inch nozzle. Pipe a 3-inch mound of pastry onto the parchment paper. Repeat to make 8 rounds. If you don't have a pastry bag, you can simply spoon the dough onto the parchment paper.

Bake the pastries until puffed and golden, about 20 minutes. Lower the temperature to 375°F and continue to bake 10 minutes more. Transfer the pastries to a wire rack and make a small incision in the side of each one to release the steam. Set aside to cool.

Meanwhile, make the filling. Pour the milk into a saucepan. With a small, sharp knife, slit the vanilla bean lengthwise and scrape the seeds into the milk. Heat gently over low heat until warm. Meanwhile, combine the sugar, cornstarch, and salt in a 2-quart saucepan. Stir in the egg yolks to make a paste, then gradually whisk in the warm milk mixture. Set the saucepan over medium heat and cook for a few minutes until thickened, stirring constantly so that no lumps form. Transfer the custard to a bowl and let cool to lukewarm, then lay a piece of waxed paper or plastic wrap directly on the surface of the custard and refrigerate for 2 hours.

When the custard is chilled and you are ready to assemble the dessert, whip the cream until it forms stiff peaks and fold it into the custard.

Slice each pastry in half horizontally with a serrated knife and place a couple of spoonfuls of the cream filling on the bottom half. Set the other half on top, being careful not to press down on the cream.

Finally, make the topping. On a surface sprinkled lightly with confectioners' sugar, roll out the almond paste thinly. With a 4-inch cookie cutter, cut out 8 rounds. Using a fine-mesh strainer, dust the rounds with the cocoa powder until completely covered. Carefully drape a cocoa-covered round over each cream-filled pastry to cover it. Serve immediately.

NOTE: The almond paste can be rolled out while the custard is chilling, and wrapped tightly in plastic wrap so it doesn't dry out. Dust on the cocoa at the last minute.

TOSCAKAKA **IS ONE** of Sweden's classic cakes, supposedly named to honor Puccini's beloved opera. It's a staple at pastry shops throughout the country, usually presented as a buttery slice of sponge cake with a crisp almond topping. And the ubiquitous version is definitely appealing. But I tasted something different at a charming bakery called Bagarstugan in Mariehamn, in the Åland Islands. Bagarstugan is housed in the city's second-oldest building, dating from 1866. It's filled with appealingly mismatched antiques, and the bakers there make Tosca Cake with fruit, the offerings changing with the seasons. I was happy to be there during blueberry time. That cake's deliciousness came rushing back to me one day when I discovered a recipe for Bagarstugan's Rhubarb Tosca Cake in Kenneth Nars's *Åländsk Matguide*. I tweaked it a bit and added blueberries. Here is the divine result.

Blåbärskaka med toscatäcke

BLUEBERRY TOSCA CAKE

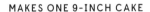

MAKES ONE 9-INCH CAKE

3 eggs

1 cup sugar

1¼ cups flour

1 teaspoon baking powder

¼ teaspoon salt

8 tablespoons (1 stick) butter, melted

2 teaspoons pure vanilla extract

2 cups fresh blueberries

TOPPING

8 tablespoons (1 stick) butter, melted

½ cup sugar

2 teaspoons flour

1 cup sliced almonds

1 tablespoon heavy cream

Preheat the oven to 350°F. Line the bottom of a 9-inch springform pan with parchment paper, then butter the parchment paper and the sides of the pan.

In the bowl of a stand mixer, beat the eggs and the sugar on medium high speed until pale and light, 3 to 5 minutes. Meanwhile, stir together the flour, baking powder, and salt in a small bowl. Add the melted butter and vanilla and then the flour mixture to the eggs, beating just long enough to combine. Pour the batter into the prepared pan and spread evenly. Scatter the blueberries evenly over the batter, pressing them down to the bottom of the pan.

Bake the cake until puffed and golden at the edges and just barely done, 50 to 55 minutes.

Ten minutes before the cake is done, make the topping. Melt the butter in a small saucepan over low heat. Combine the sugar and flour in a small bowl, then stir into the melted butter in the pan, along with the almonds and cream.

Remove the cake from the oven and raise the temperature to 400°F.

CONTINUED

BLUEBERRY TOSCA CAKE
CONTINUED

Simmer the prepared topping until bubbly, about 3 minutes, stirring only once or twice so you don't break the nuts. Quickly spoon the topping over the warm cake, spreading it evenly to the edges of the pan with a small spatula. Bake until the topping is golden and crisp, about 10 minutes more.

Cool the cake on a rack for at least 10 minutes before removing the ring of the springform pan. This cake is delicious warm or at room temperature.

VARIATIONS: In the winter I make this cake with cranberries. Substitute one 12-ounce bag of fresh or frozen cranberries for the blueberries. Toss them with 1 tablespoon of sugar before beginning to prepare the cake. Proceed with the recipe.

For Rhubarb Tosca Cake, substitute 2 stalks of rhubarb for the blueberries. Trim them and cut into 1/2-inch pieces, then toss them with 2 teaspoons of sugar. Proceed with the recipe.

THIS SPICE CAKE, adapted from *Sju sorters kakor* (*Seven Kinds of Cookies*), a classic Swedish cookbook first published in 1945, has a wonderfully delicate crumb, thanks to potato starch. As you roll the cake up, it cracks slightly, making it look like a wintertime log dusted with snow. I sometimes gather pine needles and red winterberries to garnish the platter. Try baking this jelly roll instead of a *bûche de Noël* for your next holiday party—it will take less than half the time, and it's truly delicious.

Rulltårta

 # HOLIDAY JELLY ROLL

SERVES 8

3 eggs

⅔ cup plus 2 tablespoons sugar

⅓ cup potato starch

4½ teaspoons flour

1 teaspoon baking powder

1 teaspoon ground cinnamon

½ teaspoon ground ginger

¼ teaspoon ground cloves

1 to 1½ cups lingonberry preserves or other jam

Preheat the oven to 350°F. Line a 12 by 15-inch jelly roll pan with parchment paper.

Break the eggs into the bowl of an electric mixer and beat them at high speed for 2 minutes, then gradually add the ⅔ cup of sugar and continue to beat for 3 minutes more, until the mixture is thick and pale in color.

In a small bowl, stir together the potato starch, flour, baking powder, cinnamon, ginger, and cloves. Fold the flour mixture gently but thoroughly into the sugar-egg mixture.

Pour the batter into the prepared pan and spread evenly. Bake the cake until puffed and golden, about 15 minutes; a cake tester inserted into the center should come out clean.

While the cake is baking, lay another sheet of parchment paper on a large board, or right on the counter, and sprinkle the remaining 2 tablespoons of sugar over it. When the cake is done, gently run a butter knife along the edges to release it from the pan, then invert the cake onto the sugar-covered parchment paper. Working quickly, remove the parchment paper from the top of the cake and spread with the preserves.

Beginning at the short end of the cake, roll it up to form a jelly roll. Let cool seam side down. Transfer to a decorative platter to serve.

SCANDINAVIA PUTS ITS abundant milk products to heavenly use, in custards, puddings, and creams. Sometimes they're airy, like the heavy cream whipped with a little sugar and then frozen so its crystals melt in your mouth. At other times they're dense, like the lyrically named *kalvdans* ("calf's dance"), a rich custard made from beestings, the first milk from a cow that's just given birth. This luscious Swedish cream falls somewhere in between, with a layer of froth atop a creamy base.

The dessert's Swedish name comes from the carrageen (aka Irish moss) originally used for thickening before gelatin was available commercially. The moss, which grows along Sweden's west coast, was used in many early recipes. Like a classic mousse, this cream calls for raw eggs, so be sure to use some from a reliable source. The dessert is especially lovely in summer with fresh berries.

Mosspudding

SWEDISH CREAM

SERVES 4

1 envelope (1 tablespoon) unflavored gelatin

2 cups heavy cream

3 eggs, separated

¾ cup sugar

1 teaspoon pure vanilla extract

½ teaspoon pure almond extract

½ cup crème fraîche

In a small bowl, soften the gelatin in ¼ cup of the heavy cream. Gently heat the remaining 1¾ cups of heavy cream in a saucepan over low heat, until tiny bubbles appear at the edges. Pour a little of the hot cream into the softened gelatin, whisking well to break up any lumps. Then stir the gelatin mixture into the saucepan and cook for a few minutes over low heat, stirring often, until the gelatin is completely dissolved. Pour the cream into a large mixing bowl and set aside to cool for 15 minutes.

Meanwhile, with an electric mixer, beat the egg yolks with the sugar and the vanilla and almond extracts until pale and creamy.

When the cream has cooled slightly, whisk in the crème fraîche, mixing well to make sure there are no lumps. Add a little of this mixture to the beaten egg yolks to lighten them, then gently stir the rest of the egg yolks into the cream.

Beat the egg whites until they form stiff peaks, then carefully fold them into the cream mixture. Pour the cream into parfait glasses or wine glasses and refrigerate until set, about 2 hours. Serve cold.

THIS LOVELY APPLE dessert is like a Scandi version of granola yogurt parfait. The veil refers to the cream that covers the apples. Versions of this dessert are made throughout Scandinavia, especially in Norway and Denmark, where buttered and sautéed bread crumbs—often rye—are used. Despite its elegant presentation, this is a peasant dish, a thrifty way to repurpose leftover bread. The fillings vary, from poached apples to compote to sauce. I like the texture of poached apples best.

Tilslørte Bondepiker
VEILED FARM GIRLS

SERVES 4

1½ cups rolled oats

2½ tablespoons cane syrup or unsulphured molasses

2 tablespoons butter, melted

⅛ teaspoon salt

4 large apples, peeled and cut into 1-inch pieces (about 2 pounds)

¼ cup plus 1 tablespoon sugar

¼ cup water

1 teaspoon freshly squeezed lemon juice

1 cup heavy cream

¼ teaspoon ground cardamom

Preheat the oven to 300°F. Butter a baking sheet. In a small bowl, stir together the oats, cane syrup, melted butter, and salt until the oats are well coated. Spread the oats on the prepared baking sheet and bake for 15 minutes, stirring once, being careful not to burn the oats. Transfer the baking sheet to a rack—the oats will crisp as they cool. (The recipe makes more crisped oats than you'll probably need, but they keep well when stored airtight and they're nice to have on hand.)

Meanwhile, in a saucepan, cook the apples, ¼ cup of the sugar, the water, and the lemon juice over medium heat until soft, about 10 minutes. Set aside to cool to room temperature.

Just before serving, in a large bowl, using a whisk or electric mixer, whip the cream to soft peaks with the remaining 1 tablespoon of sugar and the cardamom.

To assemble, layer the apples, followed by the crisped oats and then the cream, in parfait glasses.

THIS BELOVED FINNISH pudding is also known as "air pudding" (*ilmapuuro*) because it's so light. It's a typical after-school snack, now sold ready-made at the supermarket, though the homemade version is far superior. Your guests will have a hard time guessing what's in this pudding, but the secret is farina, which we know as Cream of Wheat. Just be sure not to use the instant variety, or you'll have a disaster on your hands.

The Finns make *vispipuuro* with lingonberry juice, which has the perfect balance of sweet and tart but, sadly, lingonberry juice is hard to find in the States. I substitute cranberry, which turns the pudding an equally beautiful shade of pink. The proportions below are carefully balanced to yield a slightly tart pudding, so you'll want to check the label of the juice you buy. Brands of cranberry juice vary from 7 to 9 grams in the amount of natural sugar they contain per serving. Seven grams will definitely make you shiver and pucker, so unless that's an experience you desire, seek out a brand that lists 9 grams of natural sugar per serving. I use Lakewood Pure Cranberry Juice.

Vispipuuro

 **WHIPPED BERRY PUDDING**

SERVES 4 TO 6

2 cups unsweetened cranberry juice

6 tablespoons farina (Cream of Wheat, *not* instant)

¾ cup sugar, or to taste

In a saucepan, heat the cranberry juice over medium-high heat. Gradually pour in the farina, stirring constantly to make sure it doesn't clump. Add the sugar and cook the mixture over medium-low heat, stirring often, until it thickens, 3 to 5 minutes. At this point you can add a little more sugar if the mixture isn't sweet enough for your taste. Remove from the heat and let cool for 15 minutes.

Transfer the farina mixture to the bowl of a stand mixer and beat on high speed until the pudding has doubled in bulk and turned light in color, about 10 minutes. The texture will be a bit like marshmallow fluff. Transfer to a bowl and refrigerate before serving.

THE ÅLAND ISLANDS are known for their malt bread and for *Ålandspannkaka*, a dramatic oven-baked pancake made with farina (what we know as Cream of Wheat) or rice. Farina is the more traditional ingredient, since rice had to be imported. Only after rice became affordable in the early twentieth century did some Ålanders begin making the pancake in a new way, but many still prefer the wheat-based version, as do I. *Ålandspannkaka* is most often enjoyed as a midafternoon treat, with whipped cream and a tart prune sauce that balances its sweetness.

Ålandspannkaka med sviskonkräm

ÅLAND PANCAKE
WITH PRUNE SAUCE
SERVES 8

4 cups whole milk

1 cup farina (Cream of Wheat, *not* instant)

3 eggs

½ cup sugar

½ cup flour

1½ teaspoons ground cardamom

1 teaspoon salt

2 tablespoons butter, cut into small pieces

Prune Sauce (see recipe, page 246)

Whipped cream, for serving

Preheat the oven to 400°F. In a saucepan over medium-low heat bring the milk to a boil, then gradually add the farina and lower the heat to a simmer. Stir constantly until the milk has been absorbed, about 3 minutes. Remove from the heat and let cool slightly.

Meanwhile, in a large bowl lightly beat the eggs, then stir in the sugar, flour, cardamom, and salt. Vigorously whisk in the cooked farina, making sure to eliminate any lumps.

Butter a 10-inch deep-dish pie plate or an ovenproof 1½-quart round baking dish. Scrape the farina mixture into the dish, smooth the top, and dot with butter. Bake until puffed and golden, about 50 minutes.

Run a sharp knife around the edges of the pie plate to loosen the pancake. Cut into wedges and serve warm, with prune sauce and a generous dollop of whipped cream.

CONTINUED

PRUNE SAUCE

¹/₂ cup pitted prunes

2¹/₂ cups water

1 cinnamon stick

2 tablespoons cornstarch

¹/₂ cup sugar

In a saucepan, soak the prunes in the water for 30 minutes, then add the cinnamon stick and bring to a low boil over medium-low heat. Cook until softened, about 10 minutes. In a small bowl, combine 2 tablespoons of the prune liquid and the cornstarch, then stir that mixture into the pan along with the sugar. Cook until slightly thickened, about 5 minutes more.

ÅLAND

The Åland Islands are a bit of an anomaly. Located in the archipelago between Sweden and Finland, they're both their own place and in between. Officially the islands belong to Finland. But Swedish is the official language, and the inhabitants are culturally Swedish. The Ålanders fly a flag of their own and are politically autonomous, which seems like a Scandinavian solution, in that it suits everyone fine. Lying as they do midway across the Baltic, the islands are visited mainly as a stopover on the ferry runs between Stockholm and Helsinki or Turku. That's a shame, because the place is truly beautiful. Nature here is virtually unspoiled, with bounteous wild plants and a distinctive cuisine that makes inventive use of produce foraged from the land and harvested from the sea. I'll never forget the acre of ramps—truly rampant!—that we stumbled upon during one woodland hike. These wild cousins of garlic would have fetched thousands of dollars in the States, yet here they were, untouched. And I'll carry the secret of their exact location to my grave.

The Ålandspannkaka pancake is substantial, offering a clue to the erstwhile harshness of life on the islands, where storms would isolate people for days. With milled wheat and dairy products always at hand, Ålanders could make this pancake without supplies from the mainland. Islanders on Gotland, off Sweden's southeastern coast, make a similarly filling pancake, but always with rice and flavored with saffron. Like the Åland specialty, it is served with whipped cream and a fruit sauce, although Gotlanders prefer the local *salmbär*, or dewberry.

FINLAND

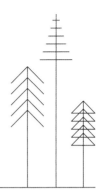

Finland is a walk on Scandinavia's wild side. Dense forests of pine, spruce, and birch cover 75 percent of the country—that's ten acres of forest per person—and "everyman's rights" ensure that people can wander and forage wherever they like, as long as they respect nature. Even though most Finns live in cities nowadays, being close to the wild remains important enough that just about everyone has a rustic *mökki*, or cabin, or at least access to one. These cabins, usually perched on the edge of water (easily done in a country of 187,000 lakes), beckon in summer and winter alike. As with the forests, access to water is a legislated right, and summer finds the lakes full of anglers hooking zander, perch, and pike to grill over alder or juniper branches. Winter doesn't mean a loss of outdoor pleasures. The Finns simply turn to ice fishing, especially in February, when the freshwater cod known as burbot congregate under the ice to frenziedly spawn. An ugly fish with slimy skin, burbot is astonishingly delicate and tasty. It might be cooked on the spot over a fire laid in the snow, or indoors in the fireplace. Or else it's tossed into a pot with potatoes, allspice, and plenty of dill to make a delectable soup.

The foods most expressive of Finnish values are those that come from the wild—the freshly caught fish, the hunted game, the multitudinous mushrooms and berries—especially if they've been personally gathered or caught, because the pastimes of angling, hunting, and foraging are as meaningful as the catch. In that regard the Finnish language is telling. The word for nature, *luonto*, originally described a guardian spirit that helps guide each person through life. If one's *luonto* was out of balance, illness could ensue. A belief in the healing powers of nature is bred in the Finnish bone.

Finland is often excluded from the larger Scandinavian family by its Nordic siblings, who cite the seemingly impenetrable Finno-Ugric language. The lack of easy comprehension, coupled with Finland's historical orientation toward Russia rather than Western Europe, has frequently led other Scandinavians to see the Finns as exotic and somehow less civilized—even though Finland was the first European nation to grant women the vote, in 1906, and the first in the world to allow women to run for public office. Even in the United States, the government in the early twentieth century sought to deport a Finnish labor activist on the basis of his allegedly "Mongolian" origins.

And then there's the sauna culture, which some outsiders perceive as extreme: naked

Finns sweating in intense heat, wearing only wool hats to protect their ears, then plunging into a cold lake or, better yet, through a hole in the ice. It's true that the sauna is a Finnish national passion, one that's central to family life. One of the great sauna rituals, besides lashings with whisks of aromatic birch leaves, is feasting on *lenkkimakkara*—pork links that sizzle on the hot rocks while you steam—or *saunasavukala*, smoked fish. Other succulent foods are prepared in the traditional smoke sauna, where sausages, fish, meat, ham, and even new potatoes are hung in the gentle smoke that rises as a wood fire, usually of alder, gradually heats the sauna rocks over several hours. Pitchers of beer, or homemade juniper beer, are part of the post-sauna experience, providing a jolt of immense pleasure as the cold drink hits your steamy body. You have to be careful to avoid a *darra*, Finnish slang for a bad hangover. It was years before anyone would reveal the source of the suppressed smiles or quizzical looks I detected when they heard or even just saw my name. *Darra* in Swedish means "to tremble or shake"—which is why the Finns adopted the word to describe the aftereffects of too much imbibing.

The Finns enjoy fire and smoke in other ways too. In northern Finland, two kilometers from the Russian border, we enjoyed an elaborate lunch in a cabin built in the style of a Sami *kota*, a tepee-like tent with a central hearth and a hole at the top for the smoke to exit. These temporary dwellings enabled the nomadic Sami to create shelter as they followed their reindeer herds. The Sami are adept at keeping the hearth fire hot enough to allow the smoke to rise, but also at taming it so they can prepare food without singeing. We feasted on Fire-Glow Salmon,

a wonderfully moist and caramelized side of salmon nailed to a plank that is set at an angle to bake in the radiant heat of the fire. Our dessert of "squeaky cheese" was baked in a cast-iron skillet on a grate over the fire, picking up smoke that harmonized with the musky cloudberries spooned over it.

The Finns' appreciation for the flavor of smoke points toward a truly distinctive taste preference—for *terva*, or tar. Finland's economy once relied on the export of "black gold," or pine tar, which was in great demand by shipbuilders. The pine trees also provided sustenance. The inner bark was stripped in the spring and dried in the open air, then baked and ground into a powder that, in good times, was mixed half and half with rye flour. In leaner times it became a loaf in itself. To produce tar, the pine trees were felled and burned in pits. The tar residue was loaded onto boats for a three-week river journey through harrowing rapids to the port city of Oulu. From there it was shipped throughout the world, but especially to England, whose maritime might depended on it. Though tar no longer flows out of Finland, the city of Kajaani is renowned for its *tervaleipä*, tar bread, whose piney scent recalls a collective past. Tar extract is also used to flavor syrup that can be spread like honey on bread or drizzled over roasted root vegetables. Finns even enjoy a tar-flavored liqueur, tar pastilles, and (naturally) pitch-black tar ice cream and chocolates. So engrained is tar in Finnish culture that when someone falls ill, a saying advises: "Sauna, booze, and tar; if these three don't work, then death will come." This cultural attribute was invoked in 2007, when the European Union sought to ban the use of tar. The Finns successfully argued that pine tar doesn't have the toxins found in tar produced from coal or oil, so they were granted the right to continue producing artisanal tar products.

Another strong and beloved flavor in Finland is licorice, though not the sweet sticks or strings that American children chew on. The Finns prefer salty-sour *salmiakki* drops, made from salmiac—ammonium chloride, an astringent salt. These candies are produced in a hundred varieties rated each year by the nonprofit Finnish Salty Liquorice Association. They are also made into a jet-black liqueur for truly hard-core lovers of the taste. Although other Scandinavians are fond of strong licorice, the Finns are obsessed with *salmiakki*.

Finland's culinary leanings toward Russia set it further apart from its western neighbors. In 1809, Sweden lost Finland to Russia after having dominated it since the twelfth century. Russia incorporated Finland into its empire as a grand duchy, and the Russian aristocracy used the country as a vacation playground, building sumptuous retreats along the Baltic archipelago. In the eastern part of the country, Tsar Nicholas I created Finland's first nature preserve. In 1845 he built a summer getaway, a charming pale pink clapboard structure with fanciful white fretwork that rises up out of the pine forest in Punkaharju, an esker ridge snaking across Lake Saimaa, Finland's largest. It was along this ridge that the Russians built a road to Vyborg to ease cross-border connections. You can now book a room, as we did, in the tsarina's villa at Valtionhotelli, surrounded by pine trees, carpets of moss, and thickets of sweet, wild raspberries.

Historically, Finnish taste preferences were divided by an imaginary line running roughly from Kotka on the Gulf of Finland to Oulu on the Gulf of Bothnia. The eastern part of the country looked east to Russia, while the rest looked west to Sweden. The greatest distinctions lay in bread baking. Eastern Finnish houses had large masonry stoves for both heating and baking, like those found in Russia. Bread was baked weekly, typically a sourdough rye with a dense but soft crumb and appealing tang. Western Finns had separate bake ovens but made bread only twice a year, usually just after the fall harvest and again in the spring when the ice had broken up. These were flat, hard loaves of rye with a hole in the center so that they could be strung on rods under the rafters to dry. Given the choice between moist, risen loaves and hardtack, it's not surprising that sour rye became Finland's most popular bread.

In addition to hearth-baked sourdough rye, Russia's culinary influence can be detected in Finland's hearty soups and in fermented foods from dairy products to pickles. It's also visible in savory pies like *kalakukko*. A specialty of eastern Finland's Savo region, this fish pie was granted Traditional Specialty Guaranteed status by the European Union in 2002. Small fish known as *muikku* are layered with fatback and enclosed in a sturdy rye crust. The oven's heat softens the fish bones, which melt into the fatback that keeps the filling moist. If the baked pie isn't opened, it can last for up to a week without spoiling, making it perfect for traveling or a packed lunch. When it's time to indulge, the domed top is removed and the filling scooped out.

Muikku are vendace, small, iridescent fish of the salmon family. Besides being extraordinarily tasty, they yield the most gorgeous tiny, golden roe, which now commands astronomical prices. The locals call vendace "the wise man of Lapland," claiming that the fish are smart enough never to swim into Russian waters, even though the lakes and rivers cross political

boundaries. One stormy August evening my husband and I went fishing for vendace on Lake Saimaa with a friend of a friend named Matti Partanen. Matti operates heavy construction vehicles by day but goes out during the long summer nights to troll for vendace in the traditional way. A large net is affixed between two boats, which slowly move through the water in tandem, scooping up fish. But as we hauled the net aboard, slowly and laboriously in the cold rain and mist, our hearts sank. Length after length was coming up empty. Suddenly a huge ball of glistening fish began to roil the surface of the water and we were heaving bucketfuls of slippery silver fish into an enormous iced container on the deck. We caught more than two hundred kilos of fish—according to Matti, merely a so-so haul. Back on shore, a handful went right into the frying pan—to be eaten heads, bones, and all. Sometimes the vendace is dredged lightly in rye meal and cooked outdoors on a *muurikka*, a large cast-iron griddle that can be set over an open fire. Or it's boiled on the spot, seasoned only with salt and a bit of butter. Vendace are so integral to eastern Finnish culture that photographers always ask people to say "*muikku*," just as we say "cheese."

Every meal includes some form of bread, the foundation of Finnish food. As elsewhere in Europe, families' fortunes rose and fell depending on the grain harvest. Barley was the earliest grain cultivated, but the Finns found that by slashing and burning their dense forests, they could get excellent harvests of rye from the ash-enriched soil. When slashing and burning was outlawed in the mid-nineteenth century, grain became scarcer, since rye didn't yield nearly as much in standard fields. Many people mixed a little of the treasured rye flour

with barley and pine-bark meal. Finland has hundreds of local varieties of bread, from Tampere's famous *rievä*, a rather flat bread traditionally made from barley flour, to *rieska*, a loaf that metamorphoses depending on locale. It can be a plump, yeasted rye loaf, a flat barley bread, or a flattish round enriched with mashed potatoes. There is even a bread known as *puolivahva* ("semi-strong"), a happy medium that is neither too strongly yeasted nor too flat. And then there are all sorts of crispbreads, rusks, and savory pies, plus a luscious repertoire of sweet breads that developed once imported wheat flour became more affordable. The butter-rich, cardamom-flavored braid known as *pulla* appears in many variations: "butter eye" buns (*voisilmäpulla*) with thumbprints of butter and sugar; cinnamon buns known as "slapped ears" (*korvapuusti*) thanks to their distinctive shape (our term "cauliflower ear" wouldn't be nearly as appetizing); seasonal Shrovetide buns filled with almond paste and whipped cream; and *bostonpulla* or "Boston cake," cinnamon buns baked like biscuits in a round cake pan. Rye bread can also grace the dessert table: an old-fashioned recipe calls simply for crumbled rye bread with fresh milk and berries.

Subsisting on basic fare is no distant memory for the Finns. Following the 1917 Russian Revolution, Finland declared independence, but Russia continued to covet its former territory. The 1939–1940 Winter War between Finland and Russia was especially brutal, for both the outnumbered Finnish troops and the civilian population. In the end Finland was forced to cede the Karelian Isthmus to Russia. But within eighteen months they were at war again, this time in the Continuation War, part of World War II's larger conflagration.

Terrible hunger ensued. Though Finland has managed to keep its borders intact since World War II, wariness about the powerful Russian bear remains. My friend Micke repeated his father's words of wisdom, which I heard from a couple of other men as well: "A Russian is a Russian, even if you fry him in butter. Don't forget this, my son."

When I first went to Finland, in 1972, to study at the University of Helsinki, the difficult war years and their aftermath were still fresh, not just in memory, but in conversation. An awareness of the unpredictable Soviets loomed large. Finland chose to behave carefully and not draw too much attention to itself, especially since the Soviet Union was an important export market. In the postwar years Finland worked hard to rebuild its economy and protect domestic production. When I was living there, that meant limitations on imports. And because Finland lacked a history of restaurant culture, few foreign foods infiltrated the traditional diet. As late as the 1980s, no durum wheat was imported, to protect Finnish-grown grain. Until Finland joined the European Union, in 1995, laws even forbade the importation of oranges until the domestic apple harvest had reached the market—a case of conflating apples and oranges.

And yet Finland for me was a culinary paradise. As the autumn days grew increasingly short, and I grew increasingly cold, I learned basic Finnish by frequenting bakeries, their windows steamy from the warmth inside. In early autumn I ordered beautiful *mustikkapiirakka* (blueberry pie) made with the last of summer's wild berries. Later my choice was sweet, cardamom-inflected *pulla*, always with a mug of hot chocolate. By December I was ordering my morning pastries in the dark as the wan sun struggled to rise by 9:30 in the morning. Needing more substantial food, I turned to *Karjalanpiirakkat*, oval pies with a tender rye crust enclosing savory rice pudding and crowned with egg butter. Loading up on carbs felt right for the climate. I later spent a few weeks with a Finnish family I'd met, entering into the rhythm of their lives. Each morning Mrs. Rissanen got up early to press fresh carrot juice for the family before going out for her daily arctic swim. (I loved that juice so much that my skin actually took on a soft orange glow from all the carotene.) One morning Mrs. Rissanen grabbed a pitcher and led me down the block to the butcher, who filled it with blood from a freshly slaughtered cow. We hurried back to the apartment, steam rising from the pitcher in the cold air. She showed me how to make iron-rich blood pancakes seasoned with green onions and topped with lingonberry jam.

Blood pancakes remain popular in Finland, and the New Nordic movement has now cast them as chic—along with other traditional Finnish foods like reindeer, rutabaga, and malted rye porridge. Meanwhile, EU membership has opened Finland up to the rest of Europe, and to the world, bringing with it a multiplicity of flavors. It is now possible to find ethnic restaurants far beyond Helsinki, in the most provincial towns. Yet even in the new, hip, and tech-savvy Finland, the country that gave us Nokia cell phones and Rovio Angry Birds, the Finns retain their taste for the wild.

LARDER

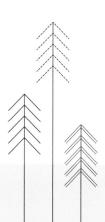

One of the delights of the North is just breathing in the air. In winter, it's crisp and scented with pine. Spring brings the musky smell of damp earth, which yields to the fragrant blooms of summer wildflowers and roses. Fall is my favorite season, when the forests are rich with the earthy aromas of the damp bark and moldering leaves that create the perfect environment for flavorsome mushrooms. The Nordic larder captures these fleeting seasonal moments. Vivid pink syrup made from late spring's tender rhubarb, when kept in the refrigerator, can evoke the joyous awakening of that season for months on end, while summer's sweetness will linger on in raspberry-rose petal preserves. Late summer's bright yellow crowns of flowering dill give fermented cucumbers a welcome herbal boost. Fresh cheese made from buttermilk, flaxen in color and flecked with cracked pepper and aromatic herbs, evokes a typical Scandinavian landscape of cows grazing in summer's lush meadows.

Today's larder is more conceptual than actual, as stocking a pantry is no longer necessary for survival. Yet the elemental flavors of the North's seasonal foods, combined with the salt, smoke, and sugar used to preserve them, still define the region's culinary identity. All of the prepared foods in this chapter are meant to accompany other dishes, and coupled with the beverages offered here, they're an easy way to add Nordic flair to any gathering. Pair your favorite meats with beets pickled Scandinavian style, with horseradish and cloves, or top them with juniper butter, with its hint of balsam. You may know how to flavor mayonnaise with garlic, as the French do, but adding spruce shoots instead transports you instantly to the northern forests.

Cardamom pods and fresh gingerroot spice up the winter holidays, in home-infused spirits that echo the flavors of gingerbread, while the first tiny birch leaves of spring create a very adult drink that goes beautifully with salty herring.

PICKLED BEETS ARE a classic example of deliciousness arising from a Nordic preservation technique. My husband and I could eat these beets almost like candy, so perfectly balanced is the sour with the sweet, but we try to save them instead to serve as a condiment with liver pâté, or as a garnish for meat or poultry. Sometimes we chop them to add to salads or the savory burgers called Biff à la Lindström (page 172). No matter how you use them, they'll add zest to your meal. If you don't have baby beets, simply slice more mature ones. These beets keep well in the refrigerator, far longer than they're likely to last unconsumed.

Syltede rødbeter

 # PICKLED BEETS

MAKES ONE 1-QUART JAR

2 pounds baby red beets

1 cup cider vinegar

1 cup water

½ cup sugar

½ cup thinly sliced red onion

2 thin slices peeled fresh horseradish

1½ teaspoons salt

1¼ teaspoons black peppercorns

2 cloves

1 bay leaf

Scrub the beets and remove the greens, but leave the root ends intact. Boil them in a large pot of salted water until just tender, about 30 minutes. Drain.

Meanwhile, bring the vinegar, water, sugar, onion, horseradish, salt, peppercorns, cloves, and bay leaf to a boil in a saucepan. Continue to boil until the sugar and salt have dissolved, 2 to 3 minutes.

When the beets are cool enough to handle, slip off the skins and trim any straggling roots. Place them in a sterilized 1-quart container.

With a slotted spoon, fish out the cloves, bay leaf, and horse-radish, along with most of the peppercorns from the brine, and transfer them to the jar with the beets. If the brine has cooled, reheat it, then pour the hot liquid over the beets to cover. Depending on how the beets are packed in the jar, you may not use all of the brine.

Close the jar tightly and leave to cool at room temperature, then refrigerate for 3 days before using. The beets keep for several months.

MY LITTLE TOWN of Williamstown, Massachusetts, was once so famous for its milk that trains carried it to New York City daily. Alas, the train service and depot are long gone, as are most of the dairies. But we are enjoying a revival of craft dairies and can now get excellent buttermilk and raw milk from a couple of local farms. Among other purposes, I use the milk to make this summery fresh cheese, whose herbal notes evoke the meadow grasses on which the cows grazed. I like to spread it on rye bread or crispbread, or serve it as part of a salad plate with tomatoes and cucumbers. Because it's tangier than fresh ricotta, it can hold its own against the robust flavor of rye.

I feel a bit guilty tossing out the whey. You could try making your own *mysost*—cheese made by slowly reducing the whey until it is brown and caramelized—or *messmör*, whey butter. Or use it to bake some bread. Luckily, no lingering sense of guilt diminishes my pleasure when this cheese is on my plate.

Piimäjuusto

FRESH CHEESE
WITH HERBS

MAKES 2 CUPS

4 cups raw milk

2 cups organic buttermilk

2 eggs

¼ teaspoon black peppercorns

Scant 1½ teaspoons salt

3 tablespoons minced fresh herbs (such as thyme, parsley, tarragon, dill, chives, and chervil)

In a saucepan, slowly warm the milk and buttermilk over low heat until an instant-read thermometer registers 185°F. Meanwhile, beat the eggs until frothy in a small bowl. When the milk mixture has reached the proper temperature, remove it from the heat, and quickly whisk a little hot milk into the beaten eggs. Add a little more hot milk until you have about 1 cup of liquid, then whisk it back into the pan of hot milk. Return the pan to medium heat and cook the mixture just until it comes to a boil. Remove the pan from the heat, cover it, and let the mixture sit until curds form, about 30 minutes.

Meanwhile, crush the peppercorns in a mortar with a pestle until they are finely cracked but not ground.

Line a strainer with cheesecloth and set it over a deep bowl. Pour the milk mixture onto the cheesecloth and let the curds drain for an hour, then transfer them to a clean bowl. Stir in the salt, pepper, and herbs. Pack the cheese into a crock or a bowl and refrigerate for several hours before serving.

WE TASTED THIS aromatic butter at Slottskrogen, a lovely restaurant at Svartå Manor in Mustio, Finland, where chef Niko Tuominen works wonders in the kitchen. He presented the butter with spelt bread whose flour had been milled in one of Finland's oldest mills—an appealingly earthy combination. At home I like to spread a thin layer of the butter on rye bread or place a dab on roasted game to evoke the Finnish forests.

Enbärssmör

 # JUNIPER BUTTER

SERVES 4

24 large dried juniper berries

4 tablespoons butter, at room temperature

Generous pinch of sea salt

Crush the juniper berries with a mortar and pestle, or chop them very finely with a knife. Mix the crushed berries into the butter, along with the salt.

THE IDEA OF nipping something in the bud is less a deterrent than a delight in Scandinavia, where early spring offers treasures that must be picked right away. Like young birch leaves, spruce tips need to be harvested when still pale green and tightly closed, since their flavors begin to turn harsh and resinous as they mature. Spruce-tip salt adds a lively, citrusy finish to roots and tubers, or it can be rubbed into meat. The mayonnaise makes a fitting crown to poached salmon. You can also layer spruce tips with dill when making gravlax, or use them to infuse vinegar or oil.

Granskuddsalt og granskuddmajones

SPRUCE-TIP SALT AND MAYONNAISE

MAKES 1 CUP SALT, 1¼ CUPS MAYONNAISE

SPRUCE-TIP SALT

½ cup tender spruce tips
(see Sources)

½ cup kosher or sea salt

SPRUCE-TIP MAYONNAISE

¼ cup tender spruce tips

1 cup mayonnaise

Freshly squeezed lemon juice,
for seasoning (optional)

To make the salt: Remove any stems or papery brown husks from the spruce tips. Place them with the salt in a spice grinder or the bowl of a food processor and whir. I like to grind the salt fairly finely—you want to avoid any whole bits of spruce. Transfer the salt to a rimmed baking sheet and let it dry at room temperature for 2 days, stirring occasionally to break up any lumps. When the salt is completely dry, transfer to an airtight container, where it will keep for months.

To make the mayonnaise: Mince the spruce tips and stir them into the mayonnaise. Refrigerate for at least an hour to let the flavors meld. Taste before serving, and add a little lemon juice if the flavor needs picking up.

THIS RECIPE IS entwined with history. Its method of pickling cucumbers is adapted from Father Hariton Tuukkanen, founder of the Pokrova Orthodox Brotherhood in Kirkkonummi, Finland. Kirkkonummi has its own history. When the Soviets had a naval base nearby from 1945 to 1956–an arrangement that Finland agreed to under extreme duress–they converted the stables on the property to a bakery. In 2001, thanks to Father Hariton's vision, and after much hard work, the stables were transformed into a beautiful church, complete with icons. The brothers also created a dining hall, where visitors can taste Russian food, including these pickles.

Before becoming an Orthodox monk, Father Hariton was a well-known chef who had worked in fine restaurants throughout the world. So he knows his culinary practices. And he swears by the black currant leaves in this recipe, which he believes are crucial to the souring process. Even with Father Hariton's considerable skill, however, pickles can be fickle, and sometimes they misbehave. As he puts it, "Sometimes the cucumbers go berserk and become too sour. Then you have to pour out the brine and give it another round of boiling, cooling off, and pouring back on the cucumbers. The souring process then ends. Too much souring will make the cucumbers soft. If this happens, you can still use the mush as flavoring in soups."

I find that if I let the cucumbers sour for only three days, they remain crisp, and the pickled garlic is a delicious bonus. Though the black currant, cherry, and oak leaves add complexity of flavor, they're not crucial to the recipe. You can enjoy these pickles out of hand or slice them onto Karelian Stew (page 176) to add some pizzazz.

Suolakurkut

HALF-SOUR PICKLES

MAKES ABOUT 2 QUARTS

4 pounds small pickling or mini cucumbers

12 cups water

10 tablespoons kosher salt

2 small heads garlic, halved

6 (2-inch) shavings of fresh horseradish

Wash the cucumbers, making sure that there are no brown spots or bruises.

Bring a large pot with the water and salt to a boil, then cool to room temperature. Meanwhile, pack the cucumbers tightly into a 1-gallon crock, standing them on end. Tuck in the garlic, horseradish, leaves, and dill stalks.

When the brine has cooled, pour it into the crock. It should completely cover the cucumbers.

5 tender black currant leaves

5 tender cherry leaves

3 small, tender oak leaves

1 large handful dill stalks, including the flowering yellow crowns, or a bunch of fresh dill

1 good-size chunk preservative-free sourdough rye bread

Wrap the slice of rye bread in cheesecloth and place it in the brine. Cover the crock loosely with another piece of cheesecloth and let sit in a cool place for 3 days, once a day skimming any foam that forms on top. After 3 days, taste the cucumbers to determine if they're as sour as you like. If not, allow the fermentation to continue (in a cold room, the brining process may take up to 5 days). When the cucumbers are ready, remove them from the brine and refrigerate for up to 1 week in ziploc bags.

THIS JAM WAS inspired by a visit to Tertin Kartano, a manor house and restaurant in Mikkeli, Finland, with acres of beautiful herbs, flowers, vegetables, and fruits that find their way into the restaurant kitchen. The estate's many varieties of roses bloom in a magical walled garden, the remains of an old stone cowshed. Their essence is captured in the lotions and soaps for sale in the manor house shop. Here I use a few fragrant rose petals to add a lovely floral nuance to otherwise plain raspberry jam. Be sure to seek out old-fashioned roses that have a strong aroma; many modern hybrids have no fragrance at all.

Ruusunterälehti- ja vadelmahilloa

RASPBERRY–ROSE PETAL JAM

MAKES THREE 8-OUNCE JARS

1½ pounds fresh red raspberries

1½ cups sugar

2 teaspoons freshly squeezed lemon juice

4 aromatic organic rose petals

Place three 8-ounce jelly jars in a pot of water and bring to a boil. Boil for 10 minutes, then turn off the heat and let sit in the pot while you prepare the jam.

Pick over the raspberries and rinse quickly. Place them in a wide preserving kettle or skillet along with the sugar and lemon juice and bring to a boil over high heat. Lower the heat to medium-high and cook, stirring constantly, until the jam has thickened, about 8 minutes. Remove from the heat.

With the back of a spoon, bruise the rose petals to release their flavor and stir them through the jam for about 1 minute, then discard. Drain the jelly jars and immediately ladle the hot jam into them. Cover the jars with lids and rings (don't screw them on tightly) and place in a hot water bath to process for 10 minutes.

Allow the jars to cool completely. If they don't seal, store the jam in the refrigerator.

THE CLASSIC SCANDINAVIAN firewater is aquavit, recognized by the European Union with Protected Designation of Origin status. This caraway-flavored drink offers a refreshing counterpoint to piquant appetizers, but sometimes I prefer to infuse my own spirits. I like to make a special birch schnapps in the spring, when the first tiny leaves appear and I can gather them from the trees. Herbaceous and peppery, it goes especially well with pickled herring.

Many Swedes seek out bitter tastes, appreciating wormwood-infused schnapps called *bäsk*, or "bitter." In consideration of most American palates, I've adapted this recipe so it has only a slightly bitter aftertaste. But if you want a more pungent drink, all you have to do is increase the number of birch leaves. And if, like some of my friends, you want an even smoother finish, you can use potato vodka instead of grain. I keep a bottle of these schnapps in the freezer, ready to pour at the spur of the moment, in the hope that a Scandinavian will drop by.

Björksnaps

 BIRCH SCHNAPPS

MAKES 3 CUPS

1 bottle (750 ml) high-quality vodka

¾ cup tiny new birch leaves (no more than 1 inch long)

Pour the vodka into a large jar, reserving the original bottle. Rinse the leaves and add them to the vodka. Cover the jar and infuse for 12 hours at room temperature. Strain and return to the original bottle. Serve well chilled.

HERE'S ANOTHER INFUSED vodka for those like me who love cardamom and ginger. For instant pleasure, keep it in the freezer.

Ingefärs- och kardemummasnaps

 # GINGER AND CARDAMOM SCHNAPPS

MAKES 3 CUPS

1 bottle (750 ml) high-quality vodka

8 ounces fresh gingerroot, peeled and cut into ¼-inch slices

24 whole cardamom pods, crushed

Pour the vodka into a large jar, reserving the original bottle. Add the gingerroot and cardamom pods to the vodka. Cover the jar and infuse for 12 hours at room temperature. Strain and return to the original bottle. Serve well chilled.

beer

FROM SPARKS STRUCK by a few hardy pioneers in the early 2000s, a new craft beer movement was soon alight in the Nordic countries. From the very outset, this movement had a different sensibility than the new beer movements in the rest of the world; it was somehow more grounded, more varied, and more creative than the rest. It burned with the energy of discovery and pride of place. It was less about just recreating the ubiquitous American-style IPA, and more about "What does it mean to be Nordic? How can we brew ... a liquid version of *ourselves*?"

Just as important, the new beers were a perfect fit for the New Nordic idea of cooking. Grapes and wine are not from this place, but these lands have sustained thousands of years of brewing. Traditional Nordic beers have always tasted of the land–smoke, earth, native grains, local honey, berries, roots, wild yeasts, bitter herbs, and the aromatic flowers of summertime.

Wine can be wonderful, of course, but beer can do things that wine cannot. It can bring powerful roasted coffee and chocolate flavors, it can suffuse the palate with an impression of burning hay, and it can bring caramel to meet the mahogany skin on a roasted bird. One beer can bring bright acid, another bitterness, and yet another a soft sweetness. Any beer can be spiced or aromatized with whatever is delicious and suits the brewer's fancy. In this, brewing is not like winemaking at all, but it is very much akin to cooking, and herein lies its culinary secret. Beer comes out of the foundation of the household, and it has always been a staple, right alongside bread and cheese. Freed from the constraints of industrial production, beer can once again taste like anything the brewer wants.

Thanks to the brewer's talent, beer can move with the land and the rest of its food traditions.

Long ago, I was a filmmaker, and once I truly understood Nordic food, I came to see it in filmic terms: Nordic food was like a Western. The conventions might be known, and the themes were clear, and not every modern plot device was available. And yet, out of this "restriction," if you were an artist, you could build a focused, towering vision. Not every movie needs a car chase, and not every dish needs Indian chiles; there are Nordic answers in families, in the history, on the trees, and in the soil, if you know where and how to look.

Does this mean that you shouldn't drink wine with any of this food? No, of course not, just as this book will not tell you to avoid cooking with black pepper. That would be silly. But through beer you'll not only find completely new pleasures, you'll also enjoy these dishes in a far deeper way. Something in your bones will tell you that *this* is the drink the food is *supposed* to be with. If you listen carefully, you will hear that voice. And if you follow it, it will be your guide into a wider world of beautiful flavors.

—**GARRETT OLIVER**, Brewmaster, Brooklyn Brewery and
Nya Carnegiebryggeriet (Stockholm), and Editor-in-Chief
of *The Oxford Companion to Beer*

THE TASTE OF rhubarb is a gift from the gods—one I didn't enjoy until I was twenty-one. I still remember the setting, my first breakfast in the Finnish countryside: a sauna, a fog drifting across the lake, a rustic shack with a rough wooden table set with a bowl of poached rhubarb drizzled with cream. A ray of sun spotlights the bowl. I lift my spoon and experience a revelation.

This drink belongs to the family of summer refreshers found throughout the Nordic countries, with elderflower, black currant, and raspberry among the most popular flavors. I generally mix the rhubarb syrup with three parts water for a subtly flavored drink, but you can play around with proportions to your own taste and think up your own uses. My husband likes to add a dash of the syrup to his gin and tonic. I prefer it uncomplicated, so that each year a sip carries me back to that initial frisson.

Rapaperijuoma

>>> **RHUBARB REFRESHER** <<<

SERVES 12 TO 14

3 pounds rhubarb (about 10 large stalks)

3 cups water

3 cups sugar

2 vanilla beans (unsplit)

Sparkling or still water

Trim the ends of the rhubarb and cut the stalks into ½-inch slices. You should have about 12 cups of sliced rhubarb. Place the rhubarb in a saucepan with the water, sugar, and vanilla beans. Bring to a boil, then cook at a low boil, uncovered, for 10 minutes. Set aside to cool to room temperature.

When the mixture has cooled, discard the vanilla beans. Strain the rhubarb and juices through a fine-mesh sieve into a bowl, pressing down gently on the fruit. (The poached fruit can be refrigerated to enjoy later; it's wonderful when drizzled with cream.) You should end up with 2 cups of syrup. The syrup will keep for at least a week in the refrigerator.

To make the refresher, mix 1 part rhubarb syrup with 3 parts water (or use a different ratio, to taste). Serve over ice.

FOR SCANDINAVIANS, MULLED wine marks the Christmas season, filling the house with wonderfully spicy smells and evoking memories of hospitality, with guests lined up at the ladle. The glogg most familiar to Americans is made Swedish style, with red wine, but in Denmark I discovered a lighter version of this warming drink, made with white wine. It's a perfect party beverage, since the apple-spice mixture can be made a few days ahead of time. Just add the wine and heat the *gløgg* before serving.

Hvid gløgg

 # WHITE GLOGG

SERVES 12 TO 15

6 cups unsweetened apple juice

6 oranges (about 2 pounds), cut into ½-inch slices

2 ounces fresh gingerroot, peeled and cut into ½-inch slices

12 white peppercorns

6 allspice berries

6 whole cardamom pods, crushed

4 star anise

4 cloves

3 cinnamon sticks

½ teaspoon coriander seeds

1 cup raisins

½ cup dried apricots, cut into quarters

2 cups dark rum

3 (750 ml) bottles white wine, such as a dry, fruity Riesling

2 to 4 tablespoons sugar

⅓ cup blanched almonds (optional)

Place the apple juice in a large stockpot and add the oranges, ginger, peppercorns, allspice, cardamom, star anise, cloves, cinnamon, and coriander. Bring the mixture to a simmer and cook, uncovered, for 30 minutes, then remove from the heat. Allow the mixture to cool, then strain it through a fine-mesh sieve and discard the solids. Rinse out the stockpot and return the spiced apple juice to it.

While the mixture is cooling, steep the raisins and apricots in the rum to plump.

When ready to serve, add the wine to the apple juice along with the macerated fruits and rum. Add the sugar, to taste, and stir in the almonds, if desired. Heat gently, but do not allow to boil. A heat diffuser on the burner will keep the drink warm.

sources

AMAZON
www.amazon.com
A wide range of Scandinavian products including *æbleskiver* and *plättar* pans; barley flour; cracked rye; lingonberry jam; licorice; pearl sugar; stovetop smokers; Swedish anchovies; Swedish candy; Swedish mustard; trout and whitefish roe.

BEMKA
www.houseofcaviarandfinefoods.com
Trout and whitefish roe.

BOB'S RED MILL
www.bobsredmill.com
Cracked rye; farina; hulled barley; light rye flour.

BROKEN ARROW RANCH
www.brokenarrowranch.com
Venison.

CAMERONS PRODUCTS
www.cameronsproducts.com
Stovetop smokers.

CAVENDISH GAME BIRDS
www.vermontquail.com
Farm-raised pheasant.

D'ARTAGNAN
www.dartagnan.com
Fresh moulard duck magret.

EARTHY DELIGHTS
www.earthy.com
Chanterelles and other wild mushrooms.

IGOURMET

www.igourmet.com
A wide range of Scandinavian products including cloudberry preserves; lingonberry jam; marinated herring; Swedish coffee; Västerbotten cheese. Also venison.

INGEBRETSEN'S

www.ingebretsens.com
A wide range of Scandinavian products including kitchenware; serving pieces; and tableware like cheese spreaders, cheese planes; and wooden trivets.

KING ARTHUR FLOUR

www.kingarthurflour.com
Baker's ammonia; barley flour; diastatic malt powder; medium rye flour; pearl sugar.

MANDELIN

www.mandelininc.com
Almond paste.

MIKUNI WILD HARVEST

www.mikuniwildharvest.com
Chanterelles and other wild mushrooms; trout roe.

NORDIC BREADS

www.nordicbreads.com
Organic Finnish rye bread.

NORDIC HOUSE

www.nordichouse.com
A wide range of Scandinavian products including *æbleskiver* and *plättar* pans; red currant jelly; salt herring; stirred lingonberries; Swedish anchovies; Swedish mustard; Västerbotten cheese.

PIERLESS FISH CORP.

www.pierlessfish.com
Fresh herring in season.

SCANDINAVIAN BUTIK

www.scandinavianbutik.com
A wide range of Scandinavian products including candy; elderflower concentrate; licorice; marinated herring; red currant jelly; stirred lingonberries; Swedish anchovies.

SCANDINAVIAN SPECIALTIES

www.scanspecialties.com
A wide range of Scandinavian products including barley flour; baker's ammonia; candy; crispbread; elderflower concentrate; marinated herring; pearl sugar; potato starch; salt herring; Swedish anchovies; Swedish mustard; Västerbotten cheese.

SOLEX FINE FOODS

www.solexcatsmo.com
Trout and whitefish roe; wild-shot pheasant and red grouse.

SPRUCE ON TAP

www.spruceontap.com
Fresh spruce tips.

WILLY'S PRODUCTS

www.scandinavianfoodstore.com
A wide range of Scandinavian products including crispbread; Norwegian *fenelår* and *pinnekjøtt*; Swedish mustard; Västerbotten cheese.

acknowledgments

Where to begin? So many people have been invaluable parts of this book!
Though my love for the North goes back many years, I rediscovered its wonders
and tastes thanks to dear friends and colleagues. In Finland, Maria Planting was
my guide extraordinaire to all things culinary and cultural; her devotion to this
project endured even after an ocean separated us, as she continued to answer
my zillions of questions about Finnish food and the language used to express
it. Maria also put me in touch with wonderful people who gave generously of
their time: Aki Arjola, Michael Björklund, Johanna Mäkelä, Kenneth Nars, Jarmo
Pitkänen, and Anna-Maija Tanttu. In Denmark, Eja Nilsson took me under her
roof and her wing, setting up meetings with the country's food activists and
tastings with Denmark's finest producers. Eja's help continued in Sweden, where
she introduced me to Jens Linder and his lively knowledge of Swedish food.
Also in Sweden, Steve Miell kindly hosted us and suggested our itinerary in the
country's far North, which included helpful meetings with Marcus Jönsson Åberg,
Eva Gunnare, and Johanna Spolander. Norway opened up thanks to the warm and
enthusiastic ministrations of Helge and Berit Semb and Bendik Rugaas.

Closer to home, my sister, Ardath Weaver, tested and commented astutely on many recipes. Stefanie Jandl also helped greatly with her meticulous testing and comments. My devoted friends Ilona Bell, Julie Cassiday, Lauren Gotlieb, Deborah Rothschild, and Leyla Rouhi were all generous with their refrigerators for leftovers and, more important, with their palates. Thanks particularly to Bodil Wilson for cheerfully answering my endless queries, and to Robin Lenz for her help with the photo shoot. Speaking of photos, I'm enormously grateful for Stefan Wettainen's spectacular photographs and Mia Gahne's lovely food styling. It's a joy now to count Stefan and Mia as friends. This book found a perfect home thanks to my fabulous agent, Angela Miller, who supports me at every step. At Ten Speed Press, great thanks go to Aaron Wehner, for understanding the beauty of the North, and especially to my talented and perceptive editor, Jenny Wapner. Art director Betsy Stromberg's lovely design contributed so much to this book. As always, my deepest thanks go to my husband, Dean Crawford, for his phenomenal palate, his amazing insights, and his brilliant way with words, not to mention his awesome back-road driving.

METRIC CONVERSION CHARTS

⋘ VOLUME ⋙

U.S.	IMPERIAL	METRIC
1 tablespoon	½ fl oz	15 ml
2 tablespoons	1 fl oz	30 ml
¼ cup	2 fl oz	60 ml
⅓ cup	3 fl oz	90 ml
½ cup	4 fl oz	120 ml
⅔ cup	5 fl oz (¼ pint)	150 ml
¾ cup	6 fl oz	180 ml
1 cup	8 fl oz (⅓ pint)	240 ml
1¼ cups	10 fl oz (½ pint)	300 ml
2 cups (1 pint)	16 fl oz (⅔ pint)	480 ml
2½ cups	20 fl oz (1 pint)	600 ml
1 quart	32 fl oz (1⅔ pints)	1 l

⋘ TEMPERATURE ⋙

FAHRENHEIT	CELSIUS/GAS MARK
250°F	120°C/gas mark ½
275°F	135°C/gas mark 1
300°F	150°C/gas mark 2
325°F	160°C/gas mark 3
350°F	175 or 180°C/gas mark 4
375°F	190°C/gas mark 5
400°F	200°C/gas mark 6
425°F	220°C/gas mark 7
450°F	230°C/gas mark 8
475°F	245°C/gas mark 9
500°F	260°C

⋘ LENGTH ⋙

INCH	METRIC
¼ inch	6 mm
½ inch	1.25 cm
¾ inch	2 cm
1 inch	2.5 cm
6 inches	15 cm
12 inches (1 foot)	30 cm

⋘ WEIGHT ⋙

U.S./IMPERIAL	METRIC
½ oz	15 g
1 oz	30 g
2 oz	60 g
¼ lb	115 g
⅓ lb	150 g
½ lb	225 g
¾ lb	350 g
1 lb	450 g

INDEX

Ten Speed Press and the Ten Speed Press colophon are
registered trademarks of Penguin Random House LLC.

Library of Congress Cataloging-in-Publication Data
Goldstein, Darra.
Fire and ice / Darra Goldstein ; photography by Stefan Wettainen.
pages cm
Includes index.
1. Cooking, Scandinavian. I. Title.
TX722.G65 2015
641.5948–dc23

2015013761

Hardcover ISBN: 978-1-60774-610-2
eBook ISBN: 978-1-60774-611-9

Printed in China

Design by Betsy Stromberg
Food styling by Robin Lenz
Prop styling by Mia Gahne

10 9 8 7 6 5 4 3 2 1

First Edition

DEDICATION

For Dean,
my companion in culinary adventure